Basics *of* Exorcism

HOW TO PROTECT YOU AND YOUR FAMILY FROM EVIL SPIRITS

Lecture given on July 25, 2014
Happy Science General Headquarters, Tokyo

RYUHO OKAWA
IRH Press

First edition, Second printing
Copyright©2015 by Ryuho Okawa
English translation©Happy Science 2015
Original title: "Exorcist Gairon"
All rights reserved
HS Press is an imprint of IRH Press Co., Ltd.
Tokyo
ISBN 13: 979-8-887370-40-8
Cover Image:©Cranach - Fotolia.com / Irina Ukrainets - Fotolia.com
First Edition (updated)

Contents

Preface 7

Prologue
Answering Questions on Exorcism 10

Question 1
How to Increase the Power to Exorcise Evil Spirits

An exorcist's power comes from his constant and daily efforts 15

Half of the battle is over when the nature of the spirit is identified ... 18

State of mind of the person or the family asking for exorcism,
also plays a part 19

If you get lost, return to the fundamental principles of Buddhism 20

Most evil spirits are people who denied the existence of the other
world and spirits while on earth 25

The source of Dharma power, the power that makes evil spirits
return to Heaven 28

In the end, fight against evil spirits by becoming one with
the guiding spirit group in the heavenly world 30

Question 2
How to Handle Spirits That Pose as Demons

If a spirit claims itself to be a demon, assess their ability
or capacity first 38

The higher the level of belief, the higher the power
to protect people 40

Pride can be a factor that prevents salvation 42

Persuade the person to throw away his pride and get back
pure faith 43

A note on cases of personality dissolution 45

Faith wavers when you are possessed by a demon 47

The necessity of considering earthly matters 49

Question 3

What You Should Do in Case
Your Ancestors Become Stray Spirits

There are both good and bad sides to memorial service
for ancestors 55

The danger of religions centered around memorial service
for ancestors 57

Ponder on the reason why the person went to Hell and talk
to him about it in your heart 59

Go to the local branches and temples if it is beyond your ability
to lead the stray spirits of your ancestors to Heaven 60

In the end, self-reflection during one's life is a requisite to go
back to Heaven 63

The need for the ability to say, "You can save yourself" 65

Why does a religion teach the teaching of self-help? 67

Question 4

Ways to Respond to People who Struggle with Mental Disorders

Fundamental solutions to issues of mental disorders do not lie in modern medical science 73

Do not lose practical capabilities and sociality even if you have spiritual abilities 75

Setting boundaries and discarding the rest to prevent yourself fromgoing insane 79

Advancement in spiritual refinement should be followed by deeper modesty and discipline 81

Hold a sense of public duty and restrain your pride 84

Institutional defense against attacks by evil spirits 86

Shakyamuni not only had spiritual powers but also the capability to deal with earthly matters 89

Nurture the ability to figure out the truth with calmness and also establish self-protection 92

Afterword 95

About the Author 97

What Is El Cantare? 98

About Happy Science 100

Contact Information 104

Happy Science University 106

About Happiness Realization Party 108

About HS Press 109

Books by Ryuho Okawa 110

Preface

It is always the season of summer that we see an increase in the number of movies and TV dramas related to evil spirits, demons and exorcism. Perhaps people want to get a feeling of natural air conditioning through its chills and creepiness. It may also be an influence from our yearly customs related to ancestral memorial services, such as *obon* and grave visits. Additionally, it is during this season that we tell horror stories, known as *kaidan*, in Japan, which may also be another source of influence.

When hearing the word exorcist, people generally imagine a scene in which a Catholic priest is in a life-and-death struggle to save a person or a family possessed by a demon. There is also a scene in the New Testament where Jesus yells out, "Get thee behind me, Satan!"

On the other hand, there is a story of the birth of evil. There was a man who vigorously fought in the name of God and the Church as a leader of the Crusades, and dealt heavy damage on the Islamic Army. But when his wife died, he uttered a curse against God and turned into Dracula.

In the context of Japanese Shinto, an exorcist would apply to the yin-yang master; in the context of Buddhism, it would apply to the monk of Esoteric Buddhism who possesses magical powers.

This book is an overview of the concept of exorcism, a topic usually considered to be a Christian subject but now given as an overview from the teachings of Buddhism. Here lies a new textbook.

Ryuho Okawa
Founder and CEO of Happy Science Group
July 31, 2014

Prologue

Answering Questions on Exorcism

RYUHO OKAWA:

Now that the rainy season has come to an end, days of extreme heat has arrived [at the time of the lecture]. I thought we should come up with a topic that would serve as a "natural air conditioning" in order to lower the room temperature by two or three degrees. In this way, we can perhaps contribute to energy conservation. Such things are trendy in the general public during this season and I thought we should give our share of help, too. Summer is a season of ghostly stories and dramas of face-offs with haunting spirits. I have given lectures on the topic in various places, so perhaps it would be a good idea to give an overview of my thoughts from time to time.

An exorcist is a person who exorcizes demons. Within the realm of Christianity, there are about 350 exorcists who have been bestowed with official approval by the Vatican. This became very famous when the movie, *The Exorcist* came out. Indeed, it is a serious matter, as even an exorcist can be defeated if the power of the evil spirit is stronger. For this reason, the matter is not as simple as to be formulated objectively and taught as a theory of skill. "Does the Pope have the ability to be an exorcist?" The answer would most likely be negative. Although the Pope may have political power, he probably does not have the power of an exorcist. The Pope does not seem to be capable of consulting this kind of problem so easily.

Similarly, for instance, staff members of Happy Science may also be consulted in their daily activities in branches and temples concerning exorcism as well as actual requests to exorcize evil spirits. There may be cases that are beyond their ability or cases where they cannot provide a complete answer. There may also be situations in which the staff have personally experienced this kind of phenomena or have some difficulties due to not being able to answer these problems at work. Perhaps there are a variety of problems.

Today, I will not give a lecture one-sidedly but answer each of your concrete questions on exorcism and complete an overall "Introduction to Exorcism." I would like to answer any inquiries related to your work or based on your experience.

Question 1

How to Increase the Power
To Exorcise Evil Spirits

[QUESTION]

At the local branches and temples of Happy Science, rituals prayers such as "Prayer for Exorcising Evil Spirits," "The Secret Key to Seal Evil Spirits" and "Prayer for Defeating and Exorcising Evil Spirits" are being held. However, we receive feedback from people who have taken those prayers telling us that their spiritual recovery is slow or that they are uncertain of the effects.

Does this mean there is a problem in how the priest is conducting the ritual prayers? Or does it mean there is a problem in a practical sense? Please give us your advice.

An exorcist's power comes from His constant and daily efforts

OKAWA:
Although spiritual discipline and acquired knowledge may be supportive to bring out one's power, factors such as the inherent power of his soul and the spirits who are supporting him, such as his guardian and guiding spirits, obviously come into play. So it would be a matter of total power.

The outcome will of course differ depending on the priest. So, devotees desperately search for those who are effective and turn to them. There is tendency for people to be attracted to places where they hear good comments such as, "My illness was cured" or "I was freed from the ghost of poverty." It is something that cannot be helped that not everyone will have the same effect. If they think that everyone is getting the same effect, there is a possibly of a misconception of some sort.

Just as a sword needs daily maintenance and care to prevent it from rusting, ultimately it is one's diligent effort that matters most. For instance, even if one becomes qualified as a branch manager, head minister or lecturer, if he neglect making constant efforts, his ability will eventually start to rust with time. Therefore, diligent spiritual discipline or refinement is necessary.

Similarly, even if one is to recite "The True Words Spoken By Buddha" [see Figure 1], the effect will differ from person to person. If a person is in a state to receive light from the heavenly world, the spiritual power of words will start to dwell within the words that they recite, creating a sufficient response in the recipient.

On the other hand, if the person who conducts the prayer is merely reading the words and is virtually in a state of no spiritual connection to the heavenly world, the recitation of "The True Words Spoken By Buddha" will not have any effect on the evil spirits. The evil spirits are estimating the spiritual power of the person, so some may even turn defiant if they see that the spiritual power of reciting the sutra is only of such level.

Figure 1.

The True Words Spoken By Buddha is the fundamental sutra of Happy Science. It is filled with soulful words from the Buddha consciousness, a grand spirit of the ninth dimension. Spiritual light is emitted by reciting the sutra.

In addition, if the evil spirits see that their power is at close contest, they may go frantic in trying to make people feel powerless by making the situation appear worse than it actually is. For this reason, even if a family, who is experiencing various negative happenings, asks a priest to come and conduct a ritual prayer or exorcism at their homes, there are some cases that the situations may appear to be in a worse state after the prayers. In such instance, the evil spirits are actually trying to cause trouble. The evil spirits are trying to make the family lose their faith by showing the ineffectiveness of the ritual.

In this way, there are cases where the phenomenon may appear as though it is getting worse. This occurs as a result of a competition that arises between the person who lead the prayer and evil spirits. Depending on the situation, one might not be able to expel the evil spirits no matter how much time passes, unless he tracks and chase down the evil spirits by himself. Therefore, it is crucial to be aware of one's ability and capacity.

There is, after all, levels to which one can and cannot save. This is an issue related to each person's calling, mission and spiritual discipline. Even though they may have similar amount of knowledge, it is for this reason that the ritual will appear differently depending on the person.

Half of the battle is over
When the nature of the spirit is identified

A few of the spiritual phenomena, such as spiritual messages in Happy Science, includes spirits of those that are not angels. By getting to know their nature through observation and studying their reactions, you will be able to identify their true form. Most of the battle is over when the nature of such evil is recognized and detected. Just like criminals of this world in hiding, evil spirits are always trying to remain concealed. They remain unconcerned while they are not at risk of being found; but they start to prepare for an escape once they are tracked down and are recognized for what they have done.

This reinforces the importance of seeing through the nature and capacity of the evil spirits; and to do this, diligent effort on a daily basis plays a crucial. It is important that you can see through the nature of the opponent, as well as their approximate capacity.

State of mind of the person or
The family asking for exorcism, also plays a part

In addition to the power of the person who conducts the prayer, factors such as faith and genuine purity of the family or the person themselves plays an important role for an effective ritual. Alternatively, devotion for spiritual discipline and a will to fight against malicious spirits in the person or family asking for exorcism are also key points in an effective ritual. Only when internal faith and external guidance respond to each other, can evil spirits be expelled.

There is also a case where the soul [wavelength] of the person possessed is very much similar to that of the evil spirit and the person's physical body has been possessed by the evil spirit for 10 or 20 years. In such a case, driving out the spirit becomes more challenging because the spirit would already feel that they have the right of residence. It's as if they are saying, "Even if a first-timer comes and tells me to get out of this body, I won't. This is my house." In such a case, it is not so easy to expel the spirit.

When an evil spirit is more powerful than the person who conducts the prayer, the spirit could possess the person who tries to expel it and cause spiritual disturbance. The exorcist would be "taking home" the spirit with him. The evil spirit possesses the exorcist and causes spiritual conflict. Depending on the level of the evil spirit, an exorcism might end up taking the life of the exorcist, just as in the movie, *The Exorcist*, where the assistant exorcist kills himself by jumping out of a window. So there are those kinds of risks and dangers.

If you get lost, return to The fundamental Principles of Buddhism

However, if you become lost, do not only think about focusing on manifesting the power of the Dharma; you need to take yourself back to the basics of Buddhism.

In Buddhism, there is the teaching of "the Seal of Three Laws" [see Figure 2], which are, "all conditioned things are impermanent," "all elements are non-substantial" and "*nirvana* is quiescence." This teaching is a very effective concept in a setting where you are trying to save a person possessed by a ghost. The teachings of Buddhism precisely provide us the method on what should be done to detach a spirit that is in possession of living out of earthbound grudges. It is just that modern-day monks, religious scholars and Buddhist scholars are not able to understand this. That is why the practitioners who are trying to exorcise the spirits must go back to the fundamental principles of Buddhism. Those principles are as follows:

All things are impermanent. Even if evil spirits and demons who are possessing a victim tries to hold on to things of this world such as their glory and prosperity, as well as their position, fortune, status and power they had while they were alive, all things in this world inevitably

Figure 2.

The Seal of Three Laws
The central teaching of Buddhism

"All conditioned things are impermanent"
The teaching that says to let go of attachments since all things change and pass.

"All elements are non-substantial"
The teaching that says all things are void and non-substantial. It is based on a thought that all phenomena in this world are temporary and that the spiritual world is, in fact, the Real World.

"Nirvana is quiescence"
The teaching that says the state of mind that attunes to higher realms in the Real World lies in letting go of all worldly attachments. This is the state of becoming enlightened. All followers of Shakyamuni Buddhism aimed to reach this state.

change. Nothing stays the same. It is impossible to keep worldly things as they are. You may be attached to your home, your children or various other things, but like the current of the river, all things flow and pass. It does you no good being attached to them. All things in this world will break apart and fall into ruin.

Just as humans grow old, pass away and are turned into ashes, structures like school buildings are also eventually demolished and then rebuilt. The same goes for business too. If we look around, a number of them go bankrupt, and only a few last more than a hundred years. Even if a business owner wants to hold on to his business and worries about it going bankrupt or his staff after his death, there is a possibility that the company has gone bankrupt already. No matter how much one worries about such things, all things will fall apart when they are meant to.

Just as bacteria break down dead bodies of humans and animals for them to return to the soil in the realm of nature, it is the same with any kind of company, institution or school. All things decompose; nothing can prevent it from happening.

In addition, the following is how the human soul should essentially be: "Do not remain attached to this world.

Let go of your attachments and remind yourself that, 'the only thing you can take back with you to the other world is your mind.' Purify your mind, return to the heavenly world and start your new training there" [see Figure 3]. This is the true original way of the human soul. Return to such pure world. It is where you are supposed to go, where you belong. In order to do go back to the pure world, it is necessary to rid yourself of earthly desires. Earthly desires are attachments to this world based on the physical body. While you are alive, factors such as money, relationships, a big house, a company, a name and other things may be useful.

Figure 3.

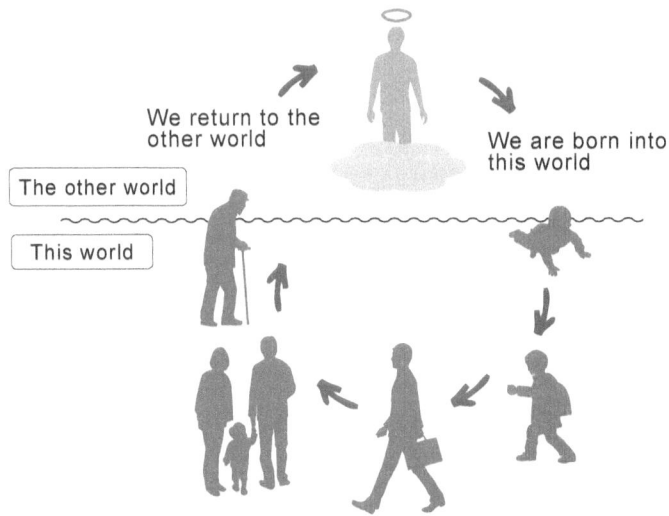

We return to the other world

We are born into this world

The other world

This world

We go through various experiences on earth

However, you must forget them all since they become of no concern after you die.

It is crucial that you train yourself to let go of those things and clear up your past. Then, your next step is to purify your mind and prepare for a higher level of spiritual discipline, so that you can move on to the next world.

These kinds of simple guidance that will help spirits return to heaven describes the teachings of the Seal of Three Laws in Buddhism. Fundamentally, we should all go back to this principle and teach it using comprehensible terms. If you can teach the principle and convince both; those who are living and the spirits possessing them, then spiritual powers will follow as you recite "The True Words Spoken By Buddha." Without being able to convey this principle, it becomes quite difficult to remove spirits that are possessing the living.

Most evil spirits are people who denied The existence of the other world and Spirits while on earth

In this world today, TV stations, newspapers and other media are reporting and releasing many contents or programs that deny the existence of the other world or spirits without any hesitation. In regards to this, we, Happy Science, are battling with this issue because if a person dies with such thoughts and beliefs, he will be left with nowhere to go after death. When people with such beliefs pass away and have nowhere to go, they begin to think that they must remain as human beings and they start to possess the living, thinking that the body they have possessed is their own residence. There are plenty of spirits doing this. Many even possess buildings and stay in offices or houses.

In order to drive away such spirits, we must guide them in understanding the principle of the Seal of Three Laws thoroughly. Or else, the spirits will not be able to leave. It would have been ideal if they had the opportunity to read even one of my books or listen to even one of my lectures while they were alive; it would serve as a hint to their awakening. However, it would be difficult in trying to preach these principles to people who haven't had such opportunities. Moreover, if the possessed person also doesn't believe in the existence of the spirits or the other world, detaching them will become inevitably difficult. The two will attract one another like opposite poles of a magnet.

There are a number of different religious rituals in Happy Science and each of them is effective. I am aware that some people are capable of driving away possessive spirits just by scaring them through performing the rituals. However, sometimes such method will not be effective enough, so it is crucial to preach the basic principle to them repeatedly.

For instance, at the local branches and temples of Happy Science, people can listen to my [recorded] lectures. If a non-member walks in and joins my lecture viewing session, he may feel obliged to listen because others will be listening carefully. But if I give a lecture at a place where people do not believe in such concepts and principles, they may start laughing out loud. It shows how careless and indifferent humans can be. Even if we try to tell such people that they will not be able to return to Heaven after they die, they are only going to tell you that they cannot believe such a thing.

Nevertheless, when such people die in hospitals, they often wander around the place as spirits or start possessing other patients. Many of them misunderstand and think that they are being confined in a special hospital room.

I often encourage my devotees to actively engage in missionary work. I may sound a little hasty and a little too demanding, but it is crucial for people to know the principle while they are alive. Even if they know some of the teachings, there are those who go to Hell or stay in this world. Still, there is a better chance of convincing them if they had known the principle before they died.

The source of Dharma power,
The power that makes evil spirits return to Heaven

However, spirits who has accumulated so much bad karma while living on Earth as human beings, is sent to Hell, and is unable to get out for 1,000 or 2,000 years, are no longer considered as just evil spirits. They are demons.

In such cases, it is not easy to make them return to Heaven since there is a possibility of them continuing to commit sins and repeat the offenses even after death. For instance, by possessing the living or driving them to insanity, suicide, murder and such. They are not easily allowed back to Heaven because they have not cleared up their bad deeds. This is like lead in water; things with large specific gravity sink rapidly. That is why such cases are harder to deal with.

When it comes to exorcising spirits of a demon-level or Satan-level, it is very difficult for our lecturers or branch managers to do so. The situation will probably be similar to hand-in-hand combat in a *sumo* match. There might not be much difference in power to "throw" them. They are quite evil, so it requires tremendous Dharma power to expel them from the people being possessed and make them go back to Heaven.

Now, then, what is the source of this Dharma power? The source would be factors such as "learning and virtuous deeds" which arise from the accumulation of learned wisdom and the "power that comes from living the right path" which springs from daily devotion and diligence to life and growth. Daily devotion and diligence lead to the strengthening of the power of character.

What is more, having Dharma power means to be able to consciously draw the flow of spiritual power from guiding spirits. This kind of power will start to produce some effect. If you feel that your power is not enough, there is also a way to drive away evil spirits by gathering your members or followers at the local branches and temples and prayer together for the target person's happiness and well-being.

In the end, fight against evil spirits by becoming One with the guiding spirit group In the heavenly world

Driving away evil spirits is quite tough. At some point, you will reach a level where you can no longer manage by yourself. This is a matter of the strength of faith and the power of the sangha [the religious group]; therefore, you cannot win unless you fight together with the whole sangha and become one with the power of the entire guiding spirit group of Happy Science in the heavenly world. There will always be a limit to individual power.

In this sense, it is crucial that you devote yourself to the Three Treasures [see Figure 4] and examine your attitude on faith. Even someone who used to be a great lecturer at Happy Science, when he leaves the group and is possessed by an evil spirit, he will no longer be able to make proper judgment and differentiate between what is right and what is wrong. When that happens, he will easily be driven into a helpless state and fall under the control of a demon. Therefore, you should be modest at all times. Live with endeavor and diligence as you hold yourselves in modesty and devote yourselves to discipline in perseverance. You will find the key to a fundamental solution in this attitude itself. There are rituals, but even before that, it is crucial that you have the ability to make someone understand and awaken him to the Truth by explaining it in plain simple language. This is very much related to the ability that one has to preach on a daily basis.

Nowadays, the number of Buddhist monks who can to preach in such ways is very small. Although they do conduct services during *obon* and on anniversaries of people's deaths, chanting a sutra in classical Chinese only for the sake of formality holds very little possibility of leading anybody to salvation.

If, for instance, a monk who happens to have a sufficient level of enlightenment chants a sutra just as a ritual, there will be powers of salvation exerted through the power in the words of the sutra. On the other hand,

Figure 4.

Devotion to the Three Treasures means for a person to accept the three treasures – Buddha, Dharma and Sangha – as sacred and for him to devote his body and soul into them. Ones who have pledged devotion to the Three Treasures are presented with the sutra books above.

monks with lower level of enlightenment will only be like a sound generator in their chanting, thus they will definitely be unable to drive away evil spirits.

If someone who knows the Truth says, "Get thee behind me, Satan!" then there will be certain power in that. But if someone who has not awakened to the Truth says the same, the evil spirits may be laughing in mockery. Since this is something that happens in the invisible world, in most cases, it is difficult to understand.

Needless to say, daily devotion and diligence is crucial; there is no end to how much you can do.

In addition to this, nurture your ability, not only as an individual but also as a religious organization. The more trust and respect the organization receives, the more power of salvation it will receive at the same time. If I were to be alone, it would be hard to deal with them since there are a countless number of evil spirits and demons. Therefore, we are not merely working to fight against many of those evil spirits. We are also working to increase the number of people with faith. When this happens, the faiths of members gather to me. This faith actually protects my powers and abilities, so such kind of power is important.

From this standpoint, it is crucial that you know and understand what it is that we, Happy Science, as a whole, are trying to do and accomplish. In addition, you should understand what it is that you, as an individual, are trying to learn and study.

It may have sounded like a general outline, but this is my answer to your question.

Question 2

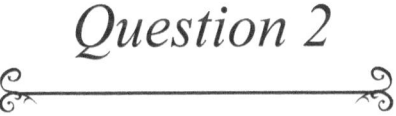

How to Handle Spirits that Pose As Demons

[QUESTION]

I would like to ask a question based on a case I have encountered. There was a woman who suddenly started suffering from hyperventilation. I thought that it might be caused by an evil spirit, and started reciting "Buddha's Teaching: The Devil-Quelling Sutra,"* with a few of Happy Science staff members there. Then, the spirit came out into the open and the woman was in a state of complete possession. Even a male staff tried to hold her down, but the woman started going berserk with overwhelming power and strength.

The woman held captive by the evil spirit started to talk and act like a completely different person, cursing us with statement such as, "This woman's life is in my hands," "You all have no power to save the world. Give up on all this salvation movement." As we started to conduct the "El Cantare Fight," it instantly released the woman out of dislike toward the ritual. But repeatedly, it kept going back in swearing, "Such rituals have no effect. You have no powers of salvation." It tried to make us feel powerless. It was then that it claimed itself to be a demon.

Then, as we conducted the "El Cantare Fight"† and recited "Buddha's Teachings: The Devil-Quelling Sutra," we started to repeatedly utter words to the possessive spirit like the following – "Ms. XXX loves Lord El Cantare. Ms. XXX is one with the Lord," "No matter how powerful the evil spirits and demons are, nothing can defeat the El Cantare spirit group," "You may be able to conquer our bodies, but not our souls!"

Just then, the possessive spirit started to release the woman. As she started to recover her consciousness little by little, we slowly started reciting "The True Words Spoken By Buddha" with her. And as she was gradually able to recite in accord with us, her heart duly recovered its balance and harmony. As she did, the degree to which the possessive spirit kept returning gradually decreased. In the end, it was when the woman was able to recite "Prayer to El Cantare" [see Figure 5] on her own, that she was finally able to completely be free from the evil spirit.

This is an experience I had before and I would be honored if you could describe to us the kind of exorcism we should be prepared for when faced with demons or lesser devils which are stronger than evil spirits, and how to create a spiritual screen to prevent them beforehand.

---

* A sutra included in the sutra book which is given to Devotee members. (see p. 31)

† Rituals of exorcism conducted at Happy Science. Included in "Prayer for Exorcising Evil Spirits" in *Prayers Book I.*

If a spirit claims itself to be a demon, Assess their ability or capacity first

OKAWA:

Listening to your episode, the spirit is clearly a demon or stronger than the demon's henchman. I am not sure of the level, but it is at least something of such level. However, demons also have management abilities; they will not try to tackle cases that are too inefficient. They will look for a well-matched case since they don't want to end up in vain. Therefore, when you are trying to assess the capacity of the demon, you can also try to look at the person whom the demon is trying to possess and drag in, and consider the degree to which the situation will have its ripple effect over others if the person falls into its worst situation. It is necessary for you to have the ability to assess the match between the demon and the person being attacked, based on their capability and so on. If you do this, you will eventually get the picture

Figure 5.

"Prayer to El Cantare" is one of the prayers included in the sutra book, *Prayer to El Cantare*.

of the opponent's ability. If you recognize what level of evil spirit is trying to haunt, then you will understand how much strength you will need in order to drive away such force.

For instance, a spirit may reveal itself as "the emperor of Hell," but a demon will not possess an ordinary devotee. Demons are not that unoccupied. Even if they say, "I am the emperor of Hell," "I am Lucifer," or "I am Beelzebub," there is no way for such demons to possess general devotees or members. They have no room to attack those people since they are "busy." They might target at key figures who will cause the whole organization to deteriorate if they were defeated. They might also aim at a person in a high position who will cause a huge confusion or split of organization if they were attacked and driven insane. If not, something of that size would not attack an average person.

Demons could be bigmouthed and like to brag, so it is important to recognize the ability of the evil spirit objectively.

The higher the level of belief, The higher the power to protect people

In this episode, the woman was lucky that the possessive spirit gradually faded away. Since the spirit said "You have no powers of salvation," etc., this shows that the being is in objection and dislike against the increasing power and influence of the organization. Thus, it is most likely to be a lesser devil.

There is also a tendency for those who were previously influenced by other evil religions before he or she joined Happy Science to be possessed like this. When people who used to be involved in other religions come to Happy Science, the possessive spirits may feel as if they lost their target by these people deciding to join Happy Science. This may be the reason for their abuse.

Within such evil religions, there are organizations that produce lesser demons. By being involved in such groups for a certain period of time, the law of inertia begins to work. Therefore, if a person who involved in an evil religion for decades gets into the stated episode, the possessing spirits would not get away instantly by having simple consultation with other members.

In this case, the issue of faith is also mentioned. Even though I have always preached the importance of faith, it has been distorted and weakened by the mass media, etc. Therefore, it has become a distant topic and something that is difficult to understand for ordinary people.

However, there is also a degree, an extent, to faith as well. From a level of "I vaguely believe," "I slightly believe," to "fifty-fifty," "I mostly believe" and to a level of "I totally believe." There are various levels to it. This increase in the level of faith is equivalent to an increase in the sense of unification with the organization and El Cantare. With deeper faith, the degree of influence on the person by our organization and El Cantare increases. Ultimately, this is an issue of which pole of the "magnet" you will be drawn to.

The reasons and causes to what a person is drawn to or attracts will vary: tendency toward materialism and evil thoughts, or other mistaken religious teachings and philosophies, or issues from one's family dynamics. In short, the situation depends on which side of the two forces is stronger and more powerful.

Therefore, even if at times you feel as though your personal strength is not enough, it is crucial to try and throw away your pride and honor. It is important that you devote yourself completely and return to yourselves as a devout believer to the organization. You should leave it all in the hands of El Cantare. In this way, the power to protect the person will strengthen even further.

Pride can be a factor that prevents salvation

Still, pride is something we all have. We all have various pride related to age, occupation, status, finance, social standing, educational background, etc.

For instance, let's assume that a principal of a school, who is possessed by an evil spirit says, "I do realize that I am possessed by a demon. I'm assuming I have been struck by it in the process of dealing with bullying issues at school." He must have pride as a principal who preaches and lectures others, so he will not be able to easily throw away his pride. Therefore, being told to "stand bare naked" is not easy. He has pride as someone who teaches others, making it difficult for him to have 100% faith.

A similar matter may also apply to police officers. They may have pride in capturing criminals, so they might think that they shouldn't be vulnerable to possession by demons. If they keep this kind of pride, they may start thinking that they shouldn't be told what is right and wrong or have their mistakes pointed out by others. As long as he holds on to such thoughts, suffering will not end. Therefore, there are influences from demons as well as how much wrong thought or delusion the person has within him. However, in another way, it is the earthly human pride we have within ourselves like a defensive armor that weakens the power of salvation and blocks it. In such cases, having a heart-to-heart talk with the possessed person is necessary.

Persuade the person to throw away his pride And get back pure faith

What is necessary is to explain to them that it doesn't matter if you have a high status at work, if you are old, have 80 years life experience, come from a family of high social standards for 10 generations, or have remarkable siblings or parents. None of these things matter because we are all individual souls. These are the things you should tell him.

If a person is able to remove such pride from himself, the spiritual light of Happy Science will flow through to him directly, showing huge effects.

In majority of cases, the person is preventing himself from being saved. Japanese people are especially imprinted a strong sense of seniority in them. This is an effect that remains from the period of Confucianism in Japan. For instance, even if a branch manager of Happy Science is trying to help a person, if he is twice as old as the branch manager, he may strongly refuse to be told what to do, be counseled, or to have to apologize.

There may also be people who are actually in need of a lot of help, but are unable to accept it because of their pride. Even though their company is not doing well, they may say something like, "No matter what you say, I am a consultant who has worked overseas. I am much more knowledgeable in management than you." Furthermore, they think it is the government policy that is causing the unwanted situation and it is not their responsibility. It is not uncommon that people are unable to realize how their self-created anxiety and stress is possibly causing them to be possessed by demons.

Pride is necessary, but it is crucial to be able to throw it away at times and embrace pure faith again.

A note on cases of personality dissolution

Nonetheless, there are cases in which a person will become dissolute when their pride is completely taken away. There are people like houses in the southern islands who, if we remove a single pillar, will break down. Just as removing a single pillar supporting a straw roof will cause the entire house to crush, the entire personality decays. Such cases are quite difficult to tackle. Although we need to remove the "rotten pillar" from them, they need to be provided with a "new pillar" as a propping pole at the same time, so that they will not collapse.

To be more precise, we need to tell them their good qualities they haven't noticed yet such as, "Other people may not have told you this before, but you have such and such excellent qualities," "you can have confidence in that" or "it is so incredible that you endured through something like that." These can eventually be made into the new pillar that acts as a propping pole that supports the ego self, while we help them to gradually remove the rotten pole.

This process will probably require a philosophy of light at its core. The method of "pouring Truth into a person while we offer support to his or her ego self" is a necessity at times. In a case where the person's ego self will go into a "melt down" and disappear once his or her "disarmament" is completed, there is danger in completing it too quickly. This is because the situation is equivalent to causing them to lose human dignity, melting away like a slug showered with salt. In a case where the person is on the verge of personality dissolution and on the edge of being admitted to a mental hospital, the previously mentioned situation is not uncommon. Complete dissolution of personality has to be avoided. It is necessary to have the process of replacing the pillar, one by one, with careful attention.

As much as it is important to recognize that a person is possessed and expel the evil, when you recognize the risk of personality decay, it is necessary to focus on supporting the ego self of the person with new materials such as a "wooden pillar" or an "iron frame" at the same time. We need to be aware of both sides of the situation.

Faith wavers when you are possessed by a demon

Any demon will gradually weaken when you establish your heart of devotion. It is because from the side of the demons, they will eventually need to battle against the whole organization and El Cantare with the whole guiding spirit group. Any demon will not be able to stay for long in this state of total enclosure.

Nonetheless, it is part of human nature that people still struggle in establishing their heart of devotion to go that far. People probably hold resistance over trivial matters. However, this is something we need to consider. That is to say, if our activities become more accepted and acknowledged in society and as we carry more influence, the power of faith and belief in people will gradually strengthen.

On the contrary, whenever the weekly magazines and newspapers mock our organization, it may cause people's faith to waver. Therefore, we need to develop our social credibility to be able to overcome such criticisms.

Demons are weird tacticians. Once a person is possessed, the demons start pointing out a number of matters such as, "Well, look at the kind of problems that your religion has. They are mistaken in this matter, and that matter as well." And as the devotee starts to think, "Oh, maybe that is so," their faith starts to wobble and waver.

Additionally, in the case of a person possessed by a demon, there are times when his family members object to an exorcism. Some devotees are unable to make a visit to the local branches and temples, because they feel really afraid to go to. Although they may be able to come as close as the nearest station, they will make a U-turn and run away back home, and gradually become unable to enter the local branches and the temples. In this sense, it would be desirable if Dharma friends [friends to learn the Truth together] could respond to such situations to give support.

Although we sometimes have tough conditions, it is still crucial to continue our work in strengthening our sangha as a whole and develop social trust and respect. We must produce more religious practitioners with higher Dharma power [spiritual power].

In general, when people are close to me, they are "magnetized" just as pieces of iron close to a magnet is magnetized. Furthermore, the closer they are to me, there is a higher tendency for them to be magnetized and there will be a stronger spiritual response. On the other hand, when a person who used to be close to me becomes more distant through personnel transfer, the magnetic strength will weaken in spite of their previous closeness.

Such matters should be taken into consideration as an important matter as we try to proficiently strengthen our unity as a religious organization. This will definitely be related to the powers of the Education and Training Division, the El-Cantare Belief Promotion Division, and other numerous related powers at work in support.

The necessity of considering earthly matters

There is another factor to be taken into consideration. This is especially true for lay members, although the same thing can happen to the renounced [staffs] as well. It is not uncommon for unresolved earthly problems to become actual causes for people to be attacked by demons.

Although we are usually against materialistic issues or earthly things. However, if the worldly logic and earthly causes are making the devotee stumble and unable to solve his or her issues, and is unable to proceed due to distress, then it is the worldly issues he needs to settle. We must think about how to exert our wisdom to resolve those issues.

For instance, if a CEO of a medium-sized business with an annual turnover of one million dollars has an immense debt of five million dollars, he will probably struggle to fall asleep every night. How is the person to return a mammoth debt of five million while there is only an income of one million? It is not an easy amount to pay off.

If he will somehow take specific measures such as changing company culture, changing its earning structure and reducing the debt, and if the efforts go into orbit, the demons become easy to defeat. However, if the situation is as hopeless as, "If things stay as it is, there could only be breakdown," there may be no way of escape. Therefore, if something needs to be settled on an earthly level, that is what should be done.

Additionally, an illness may well cause our hearts to weaken and be vulnerable. If that is the issue we are faced with, we must try and cure the illness. If there is no cure, we must try to take a philosophical view on life and take every measure to face the issues that come with it so that we won't leave behind any troubles for our family members. Sometimes putting our affairs into order will lead us to feel still and stable.

As we can see from these examples, it is crucial to take appropriate steps to practically resolve what can be resolved. These points can sometimes be our blind spot. In Alain's *On Happiness*, there is a story of a baby who wouldn't stop crying and the nanny claims it must be hereditary since the father and grandfather used to be the same. However, it turned out the baby was crying because a pin inside the baby clothes was rubbing against the baby's skin. As in this particular story, a lot of people misunderstand certain phenomena by not being able to realize the actual origin of their issues.

Even when we are trying to solve a spiritual issue, there are times when it turns out to be an earthly issue and that was where the person's "pain" was coming from. Just like the baby in Alain's *On Happiness*, he will stop crying if we remove the pin.

In the same work, Alain also tells a story of Alexander the Great's horse. Alexander the Great saw a horse go into frenzy, but he immediately saw that the horse was only terrified of its own shadow. As he guided the horse to face toward the sun, the horse calmed down.

Accordingly, it is crucial to be able to see through if there are any earthly causes. Just being spiritual is not enough; having insight into the earthly cause is what is needed. If we go back to the example of the CEO of a mid-sized business with a debt, the main cause of the situation may not exist in CEO himself. But in his wife, his children, or somewhere else that even the CEO is not aware of instead. There are also cases in which the CEO does not talk about the cause. Or, there could be someone else in the company who may actually have problems. If there are causes that one is unaware of, it is important for him to do his best in exploring it.

I have explained from various different angles, but in the end, it will be an "all-out battle."

Question 3

What You Should Do In Case Your Ancestors Become Stray Spirits

[QUESTION]

I would like to state my question from the viewpoint of memorial service for ancestors. When families are faced with serious obstacles, such as unexpected accidents, bankruptcy, and other misfortunes, these are sometimes said to have something in relation with the ancestors who passed away. Is there a way to conduct methods of exorcism from the perspective of memorial service for ancestors?

There are both good and bad sides to Memorial service for ancestors

OKAWA:

I believe there are both sides to memorial service for ancestors. In fact, parents and grandparents who passed away may wish to be properly mourned and respected. This kind of feeling could be stemmed from human affection and attachment. However, there are certainly cases in which the spirits of the ancestors who have been cast to Hell, turns to their descendants for help because they, themselves, do not know what to do and become what we call "possessing spirits." This is the problem. Depending on the religious group, some may say that there may be constant misfortunes because your ancestors have gotten lost and became stray spirits. Sometimes this is correct. Unless people make the lost spirits of their own ancestors return to Heaven, there are cases in which they will never be able to become healthy, their business will not go smoothly and family relationships will not work out.

While I am aware of religious groups that are trying seriously to grapple this issue, there are groups that use memorial service for ancestor as a means of shifting the blame. If people put all the responsibility onto the ancestors, it allows decedents to blame it all on them.

For the religious group, it becomes a "cure-all universal remedy," allowing them to be able to solve anything while completely ignoring earthly problems.

I guess many of your parents are still alive, but if we go back to your grandparents' generation or the generation before that, the case would be that most of them have passed away. Therefore, if one is told that an ancestor from a number of generations ago is haunting him, that person will probably feel very hopeless. Depending on the person, if he is told, "An ancestor of the maternal side from three generations ago is haunting you," he may feel like giving up. The person will be told to pray anyway or keep holding a memorial service for his ancestors every month. As they keep going to that religion, he will be imprinted with those words and will be veiled with gloomy thoughts, causing him to be possessed by evil spirits in the end.

Then, every time the person attends any service of that religion, he will be possessed by lost spirits, taking home with him spirits that are not even his own ancestors. Some people become as though they have been soaked deep in coal tar. I will have to refrain from mentioning any group names, but some of the religious groups which focus on holding a memorial service for ancestors have this kind of nature in them.

The danger of religions centered around Memorial service for ancestors

I remember a time when I tried to do research on a particular religion. I asked a member of Happy Science, who was previously a member of that religious group, to lend me some books and sutras. However, I immediately let go of it as it was shrouded with foul spiritual energy. Sutras and the books emitted so much creepy energy. Like dioxin, it was emitting some spiritual energy that was poisonous. All the books, sutras to their books on their basic teachings, emitted something poisonous. It clearly means that there was some major mistake in the makeup of the group.

It is very likely that there are factors of lie, falsehood and fraud within the mind of the people doing the management. This means that there are a number of deceived followers in the group. They are made to take the memorial service for "ancestors" for those who are most likely to be many kinds of unrelated evil spirits. Lost spirits, out of pain from their sufferings, pose as ancestors to encourage memorial services. Then the followers will be told by the core members of the religious group that the lost spirits are ancestors of the followers, and that they are possessed by those lost spirits, in order to induce more services. However, in many cases, the more memorial services for ancestors that they hold, the more evil spirits gather.

This is what will happen if the leader of the religious body lacks power or Right View [right understanding], so you can see that there are both right and wrong to memorial service for ancestors.

As I taught in the early days of Happy Science, it is crucial to begin by correcting and reforming the lives of people who live in this world. It means to establish a mindset to read the books of Truth as well as to develop an appropriate stance of leading a righteous and spiritual life. At Happy Science, various ritual services and ceremonies are held at branches and temples. Therefore, in that regard, it would be best to take part, and pray together with priests and conductors. It is a safer way. This is what I preach at Happy Science.

If the religions based on memorial service for ancestors encourage their followers to conduct prayers for ancestors at home every day, day and night, this increases the risk. This is because it could sometimes attract spirits unrelated to the ancestors of those followers. There is no need to conduct a memorial services for those ancestors that have returned to Heaven. Rather, the ancestors are in a position to guide their descendants whenever they are in need, so remembering them for their good old memories time to time will make them happy. We don't have to go as far as to offer them three meals a day [like the custom of holding memorial service for ancestors, seen in places such as Japan]. This is only for ancestors of those people that have returned safely to Heaven.

Ponder on the reason why the person went to Hell And talk to him about it in your heart

If the ancestor spirit is in Hell, he is unable to accept any offerings. For example, this applies to a so-called hungry spirit. Just as it is said, "anything a hungry spirit tries to devour will burst into flames," he is in a state where he cannot feel content whatever he puts in himself. Furthermore, there are some that become a cluster of desire where nothing is enough for them and continue to ask for more prayers, services and offerings to be made. These spirits can be unrelated to our ancestors, or they may sometimes be our actual ancestors.

This is something that can be made clear to some extent by looking at the ancestor's reputation in his family and relatives. If we listen to them talk at the funeral service, we would be able to conclude to some extent whether the person was heavenly or hellish. There is something we can understand through public opinion. In most cases, the guesses that people make about whether the deceased person has returned to Heaven or not are correct.

In such cases, just as I previously mentioned, it is important for the descendants to ponder why the ancestor is lost, and once is it made clear, communicate these as a concentrated thought to the spirit within the mind of the descendants. This can perhaps be done during any of the ritual services for ancestors held by Happy Science, talking to them through our mind, "You are probably mistaken on this part. It is better if you correct it." Advise them these things in ways they can understand through the heart, in addition to reciting sutras. If the spirits of ancestors are willing to listen, his thoughts will eventually reach them.

Go to the local branches and temples
If it is beyond your ability to lead
The stray spirits of your ancestors to Heaven

There is one thing we need to take into careful consideration. It is when your ancestor claims that holding memorial services for ancestors is the duty of the descendants and that he is lost because of the descendants' lack of service. If we continue to tolerate such a situation, it gets harder for the ancestors to reach Heaven.

It is just like modern-day China and South Korea, continuing to blame all their present unhappiness on what Japan did to them in the past by saying, "We are under such conditions because Japan was bad." This attitude will never allow them to reach Heaven. How they state it is very similar to what a spirit, that will never reach Heaven no matter how many memorial services for ancestors are done, would say.

The same thing applies to ancestors who put themselves in the same situation against their descendants by saying things like, "I am unable to reach Heaven because my descendants do not properly pray for me." Such ancestors will not have an easy road to Heaven. They are required to practice self-reflection.

In the world of Hell, there is the function to force the lost spirits toward self-reflection. Hell is, indeed, an uncomfortable and unpleasant place. When a person in Hell takes a look around, he is actually surrounded by people that are similar to them. If a person is an egoist, he would usually possess only positive self-image and, since people can recognize the quality of others very well, others around will not appear as good people. By looking at others who live in the same world as he does, he is able to recognize, "I don't want to be like these people." In the process of having seen people who he dislikes and various other people every day, he starts to want to leave such a world. Getting into this kind of mindset will be a trigger for him to leave Hell. In this sense, Hell collects people akin. It is the same thing in Hell; like attracts like and they gather together.

For example, in the Ashura Realm where violent people like gangs gather, there are bloody fights on a daily basis. However, if one roundly experiences such sights every day, one day he would want to leave and cut ties with such realm. This becomes an important chance for him to leave. At such times, spirits from Heaven sometimes come down to save him. If his descendant is involved in a righteous religion and in activities of faith, this may send off a helping light and the angels may support his salvation. Memorial service for ancestors, in this sense, is important.

If I were to mention something for the sake of safety, for instance, if we are to save people who have fallen from a boat and are drowning, we can probably assess how many of them we can save. If one is a woman, she can calculate how many people a woman's arm can lift on board. Furthermore, if one tries to take on board too many at once, the boat would eventually capsize and sink, unable to save any of them.

Hence, it is crucial to be aware of one's strength and ability. If one sees that it is beyond his capacity, he should ask for support at a local branch. If the help of a local branch doesn't feel enough, he could go to a big temple and ask to have prayers be done and services together with him. By joining hands together, the "boat" will be bigger and salvation becomes easier.

It is important to know that there are both sides to consider in memorial service for ancestors.

In the end, self-reflection during one's life is A requisite to go back to Heaven

Some selfish parents may claim that the children's disrespect and disobedience are the cause of their unhappiness in Hell. Such an attitude will prevent them from leaving Hell. Although there may be matters such as parent-child entanglement, etc., as there is the law of cause and effect, the eventual responsibility returns to each individual. Even if a group of people is placed in the same situation, it is possible to make different choices of thought and action as an individual. Therefore, there is no reason that a parent should go to Hell even if the child is a failure. Even if one's child is full of faults, it is possible for a parent to have his own way of thinking or living. It is likely for the parent to be influenced and dragged into the child's issues, but it is definitely possible to return to Heaven by recovering one's life in his own way.

Ritual service for ancestors, without a doubt, still holds its importance but it is equally important to teach them this: "In the end, it is themselves who need to well understand the law of cause and effect; they need to realize that there are things they need to reflect upon within their behaviors and actions during their lifetime. They won't be able to reach Heaven unless they examine themselves." If they struggle to understand, then we must put the teachings into practice as a role model. If the lost spirit sees his children and descendants practice self-reflection, he who haunts the descendants will start to see what it is they have to do, saying, "Oh, I see. That is how you do it." They start to get the idea and actually start to reflect on themselves.

In this manner, religious groups which focus their teachings on holding memorial service for ancestors have an overall tendency toward having a viewpoint that places responsibility and blame onto others. For this reason, they should be careful since such groups may have become mistaken religious organizations [evil religions]. Memorial service for ancestors cannot be an unconditionally and completely good. If the style of the ancestor service contributes to increasing selfishness and the ego of the ancestors, the service may end up nurturing the evil part of ancestors. There is also the possibility for a lot of unrelated souls to be drawn toward the descendants, wanting to be prayed for and making them suffer. Therefore, it is definitely crucial to know your capacity well.

The need for the ability to say, "You can save yourself"

Shakyamuni had a very rational side and some of his teachings were seemingly cold. This flows throughout the teachings of Buddhism. It is important that we hold a very cool side within us at times. If one is just too emotional, he will be depended on by an overwhelming number of spirits. If spirits keep coming and asking for help, it will be beyond his strength and capacity. Salvation is important, but we must be able to understand the philosophy to teach that self-help is partially necessary because of the law of cause and effect. We must have the power to say to our followers, "You can save yourself." You must not think that everyone can be saved from the outside power. We might ruin ourselves unless we are able to embrace the cool and rational side of us as we approach our case.

There are Buddhist monks who preach about self-power and outside power, but the degree of their enlightenment will depend on the degree of spiritual experience. Shakyamuni preaches something like the following in the Agama Sutras – "if one throws a heavy stone into a pond, will it float? No, it won't. It will sink. Similarly, if one has accumulated wrong deeds during his lifetime and are thrown into the 'pond,' he will sink. Now, if we pray for the stone to float, will it then float? No, it will not be so."

His way of explaining sounds a little bit cold, but in short, there are compensations or debts each person has to pay. Buddhism teaches that matters don't come to an end unless one finishes redeeming the debts from his past.

Why does a religion teach
The teaching of self-help?

What I have spoken of so far is the reason why Hell will not completely disappear very easily. While there are people who have come out of Hell, there are a number of them falling into Hell one after another. And the root cause lies within this world.

There are a lot of people in this world who are living a mistaken way of life. A number of people are living under mistaken thoughts for a number of decades. Thus, the population of Hell continues to grow. In fact, there are people who return to Heaven out of being disgusted with Hell; on the other hand, as I have previously stated, there are people who fall to Hell. The reason behind them going to Hell is the same principle of the relationship between a stone and water. They sink because they weigh heavier compared to "water" and that weight is the weight of their own karma [bad thoughts or deeds]. Hence, this is something that individual needs to solve themselves. Since these things can happen, Happy Science has kept the teaching of self-help as part of the teachings.

Although, in other countries, if a group presents itself as a religion, there will be people who say such things as, "A religion preaching self-help? No way. There will be no need for religions then" or "If things can be done by self-help, this will be 'selfism' and there won't be the need for a religion." If true salvation has indeed been realized by outside power, then there would be no need to preach about self-help. However, I am aware that Hell is continuously growing in its population. Such people are not supposed to be easily saved through outside power. Since they create reasons they fall into Hell by themselves, until they come to this realization, it takes time for them to be saved.

It is crucial to educate people to save themselves. It needs both sides; outside as well as self-power. As much as outside power is important and mighty, so is self-power. Matters such as ancestor worship are considered outside power and I wouldn't say it is unnecessary. It is necessary, but it is also important for the lost spirits in the other world to be aware that they, themselves, can put an end to their wrongdoings.

Therefore, how much one has studied the Truth will ultimately become the base. If one has understood the Truth well and enough, he will be able to present the Truth in a way that is appropriate for the other person.

Remember to be cautious of religious groups that are persistent and single-minded with holding memorial service for ancestors. They are likely to lose sight of the importance of self-responsibility. Therefore, you should watch out for this kind of religion.

Furthermore, please tell people about the reason why Happy Science is preaching the concept of self-help.

Question 4

Ways to Respond to People Who Struggle With Mental Disorders

[QUESTION]

I would like to ask about how to prepare ourselves and respond to people with mental disorders such as schizophrenia, multiple personality and intense spiritual disturbance.

Fundamental solutions to
Issues of mental disorders
Do not lie in modern medical science

OKAWA:

This issue definitely gets very difficult depending on its degree. Indeed, this would be a tough issue. As I have mentioned in the previous question, if the degree of issue goes to the extent where the main pillar is rotten, it is extremely difficult to retain the original form of a house and maintain a unified personality. Such cases are extremely difficult. Sadly, there isn't an end to the number of people who are defeated in life. We are all faced with many challenges and trials throughout our life, but there isn't an end to the number of people who are defeated and disappear beneath the waves.

Although medical science is trying to tackle issues of schizophrenia and multiple personality, they don't seem to be offering any fundamental solutions. Basically, they have responded by keeping the patients in isolation, so that they will not cause any trouble to other people. They have also prescribed tranquilizers, so that the patients themselves will not go into rage too much.

However, when we say "multiple personality," it is an issue of how we use this phenomenon. For instance, since I can take in various types of spirits inside of me and my personality changes according to those spirits, it can be said that I have a multiple personality-like aspect. However, I do not have any problem in my case because I have a firmly built "control tower" at my core. On the other hand, if there is no firm control tower, one's personality will be taken away completely and he could turn into an entirely different person. In, fact, it is definitely unusual and abnormal if a person goes on living in such a state. Although the difference between the two situations seems very small, there is a difference.

This situation is described in our recently published book, *Tenrikyo Kaiso Nakayama Miki no Reigen* [Spiritual Messages from Miki Nakayama, Founder of Tenrikyo] (Tokyo: IRH Press, 2014). There was once a time when the spirits of ten gods came down to her one after another and she started roaring with a man's voice. This must have been a very scary experience for those around her. They decided to lock her up in a warehouse. This is equivalent to the situation as when a mentally disturbed patient is confined in a hospital.

Although the spirits that possessed her were neither evil spirits nor demons, but of a high spirits, it seemed as though she had lost total control from the viewpoint of ordinary people. It probably looked as if she was showing symptoms of multiple personality or schizophrenia. Regardless of good or bad, there is enough possibility for such phenomena to take place from a spiritual meaning.

Do not lose practical capabilities and sociality Even if you have spiritual abilities

In Buddhism, this applies to the last of the six divine powers [see Figure 6] – *rojintsu* [The ability to extinguish physical desires by the power of higher wisdom. It is also the power to be able to live as an ordinary person while maintaining psychic abilities and as a great person of common sense]. To be more precise, if one just feels too grateful for his psychic and supernatural powers and simply encourages himself to keep moving forward, he will definitely get carried away. Although a person may possess a high level of psychic abilities, it is crucial that he sustain his abilities to make decisions, to work and to be practically capable. This is an essential discipline for a person to keep his sanity. It is important to make this discipline serve as a balancer to prevent the personality from breaking down.

Upon this, I usually encourage all of you to study well. For instance, some of you may think it is somewhat

Figure 6.

The Six Divine Supernatural Powers
The six superhuman powers in Buddhism

Tengen / Clairvoyance

> The ability of spiritual sight. Allows one to see through the aura and possessing spirits of living people; also allows one to see through the other world and to know the condition of people's reincarnations.

Ten'ni / Clairaudience

> The ability to hear the voices of spirits in the other world.

Tashin / Mind reading

> The ability to distinctly understand what's in other people's minds and to feel their emotions as if they were one's own.

Shukumyo / Fate reading

> The ability to see one's own future; it also includes the ability to distinctly see through fate and past lives of others by reading their thought tape.

Jinsoku / Astral travel

> So-called "out-of-body experience." The ability that enables the soul to leave the body behind on earth and teleport and travel to the cosmos and the spiritual world.

Rojin / Spiritual wisdom

> The ability to extinguish physical desires by the power of higher wisdom. It is also the power to be able to live as an ordinary person while maintaining psychic abilities and as a great person of common sense.

[Refer to Ryuho Okawa,*The Laws of the Sun* (New York: IRH Press, 2018).]

strange for a religious group to study English vocabulary. Certainly, English is something people try to improve in order to succeed more in society. It can actually support your mental health and help restore balance within you as well.

Additionally, for example, I previously spoke negatively of the mass media. There are, in fact, disgusting matters in the newspapers, TV, radio and the weekly magazines. But to be informed of what is going on in the world through the news etc. and getting to know various things will help you understand the law of cause and effect. They present you with situations that show, "If you do this, that is what will happen."

For instance, if you watch the news on TV, you can understand matters such as "taking a little girl out for a day in a car just because she is adorable" would be considered a crime and will cause an uproar. In this way, you can understand that such things should not be done. However, if you do not know these things or haven't touched on it, you may think it would be fine if you explained, "I thought she was so adorable and decided to take her out in a car with me to play. I didn't mean any harm." By watching and checking the news etc. of this world, it would enable you to maintain a balance.

In this sense, although reading various novels in a well-balanced manner can do no harm, it will become problematic if you only read novels about killing and murder. It might lead you to start researching about crime in secret or start putting up pictures of dead bodies in your room. Therefore, in order to prevent yourself from becoming like this, it is extremely important that you maintain your social and practical capabilities. You need to be aware of how the public opinion will view things just in case. It plays an important factor as a balancer. All of these apply to the power of rojintsu. If you use your supernatural powers too much and isolate yourselves too much from this world, it can be a sign that something strange is happening. So for the sake of preventing yourselves from such phenomena, rojintsu is something you should be aware of.

You should not deny everything of what is in this world. You can avoid becoming insane by partially adopting what is effective into your daily practice. This is important. There is danger involved in neglecting your daily practices and focusing too much on the spiritual side.

Setting boundaries and discarding the rest
To prevent yourself from going insane

Even high spirits could have the power to destroy personalities at times, so you should be cautious, just in case. There are times when the energy of the spirit gets more powerful than the capacity of the person or when the spirit fails to appraise the capacity of the person. High spirits approach a person expecting to use him as a "vessel" to carry out certain tasks. But if the soul of the person is not powerful enough for the mission, the pressure may turn the soul into a boat made of mud that sinks. There are tasks and mission that require much more power and strength than what the person has. In such situations, the ability to discard is necessary.

After all, we are human beings living in this world and not the other world, so we need certain wisdom to survive as beings in this realm. This wisdom is the ability to tell apart boundaries and discard what is unnecessary.

You should set proper boundaries by drawing a line that says, "It's doable for me up to here, but not from here on." For instance, there are boundaries in how much responsibility one can carry and bear within the family. It is the line that says, "This is how much responsibility I can carry within my family. I can be responsible of this much as a father or as a mother, but it is a little difficult beyond here." It would be natural for a mother to be dedicated to her children's education, but a mother must also know that there are limits and boundaries to the child's abilities. Therefore, she needs to be able to practically let go of her wishes and expectations at times by just thinking of it as a secular matter.

Sometimes there are people who say things such as, "There is no meaning to life if I do not fulfill this dream." This is a bit too extreme and there is a possibility that such people will become spiritually disturbed. If a person's spiritual disturbance reaches its utmost, there are times when the symptoms will be medically diagnosed as an illness or a disorder. However, there is a point of no return where there is no hope for any recovery once it is reached; we need to offer a course of correction before he is even near that point.

If you become too spiritual, and your daily lives start going funny, those should be corrected. You will need to shift your focus much heavily on the ordinary part of life that average people lives by. Alternatively, if you have boundaries that you must protect for the sake of your family, you must make efforts to achieve it.

Advancement in spiritual refinement should be Followed by deeper modesty and discipline

When people start hearing voices of spirits, they will probably be curious in the beginning and listening attentively. However, as time passes, the content of what the spirits say will gradually start to change. The spirits will start talking about various matters, and as the content slowly changes, it gets hard to tell it apart. At first, you think the voice is that of a high spirit, which it may well be, but the content will gradually start to be replaced by something else.

Let's use the chief editor of *The Liberty* as our example here since he is just sitting right there [audience seat]. Let's say the chief editor of *The Liberty* hears voices of the spirits from the heavenly world. The voice says, "*The Liberty* is a magazine that can save the world. Whether the world can be saved or not is all dependent on your power and strength." The chief editor will think, "Yes, indeed. I also think so." And the spirit continues saying, "So study well, write good articles and enlighten the world. You can save the world." Therefore the chief editor would think, "Indeed. That is exactly so. This must be the words of an angel." Then about a month later, the chief editor hears that voice again saying, "Your power is much greater than *Asahi Shimbun* [one of the five national newspapers in Japan] and NHK [Japan Broadcasting Corporation]. The world is all up to you, all in your hands." The chief editor would say, "Yes indeed, it is," and starts following that voice. He will eventually start making statements that are slightly "off the mark" in the light of common sense and it all gradually starts getting strange.

Therefore, it is crucial to hold both subjective and objective view of things. It is fine while he is able to see that there is the relationship of power among other newspapers and magazines and that they have power and capacity to some extent in this world. However, he will completely lose the ability to view things fairly and objectively only when his view of the world becomes so narrow, allowing him to only be able to see what is in front of him like a blindfolded carriage horse. In short, it means that spirituality should equilibrate with our worldly practices after all.

Of course, there is a form of spiritual discipline whereby you practice religious seclusion for a certain period of time for the purpose of enhancing one's inspiration, mentality, etc. Although there are various ways, there won't be much risk if it is practiced under a fixed set of established methods. While it is possible for a person with a prominent soul to have the power to endure the solitude, it is often unbearable for an ordinary person. He will be tempted by various whispers of the devil during his training.

It is said that in *Sennichikaiho* [walking meditation practiced around the mountain for a thousand days], one starts hearing various voices during the night and traps of temptation appear. Indeed, such situation would make people become vulnerable to be possessed by various spirits. Other disciplines such as fasting and not drinking water are also included in the training. Therefore, the phenomena of various hallucinations as well as traps of temptation are induced a lot, so there are these types of difficulty in such disciplines [Refer to Ryuho Okawa, *Sakai Yusai Nihon Tendaishu Dai-Ajari ni Indo wo Watasu* (Guiding the Soul of Japanese Tendai Sect Master Yusai Sakai)(Tokyo: IRH Press, 2013)].

Whether a person is to be endowed with psychic abilities or not, is something I cannot precisely say since the time it takes for that to happen depends on each person. Of course, there are possibilities, but even if the channel opens, one should not rejoice in unconditional delight; you need a certain level of capacity that is suitable and appropriate to the psychic abilities.

In other words, if I were to exemplify the psychic powers as a tool to research the depths of the sea, psychic powers are used as the weight to dive deep. However, you will need the power of buoyancy equal to that to be able to come back up to the surface again. It is crucial to practice spiritual refinement in order to nurture such ability within ourselves. Therefore, the more you advance in your discipline, the more important it is to be modest and devote yourselves.

Hold a sense of public duty and restrain your pride

Just as it happened within Happy Science as well, if a group expands and the work load increases more and more, there would be times when a person cannot withstand the amount of responsibility on his shoulders. It is often at times like this that the person's ego self or selfishness is so strong and may feel as if other people are doing something bad when something negative happens to him. This is when the importance of a sense of public duty is required.

It is necessary to have the capacity to accept the situation by putting oneself aside for a while and prioritize what is best for the whole group. This is a crucial point.

The demons are always prepared to attack by taking advantage of your unguarded moments of vulnerability. Without holding a sense of public duty and restraining pride, people are sometimes defeated by demons.

Recently, in Happy Science, staff members with psychic abilities have been emerging. The fact that they just happened to have psychic abilities could help the organization for a certain period. However, if the group is to expand globally, there will be an increase in the scale of management and administrative affairs. Should the occasion arise, strength in a secular sense will be needed. Unless each of you have the strength to correspond to wider ranges of earthly affairs, there will be difficulties in operating the institution.

If not, then we might start getting staff members who are unable to respond to practical matters in spite of how much they were able to develop their psychic powers. Should that happen, there would be an issue as an organization on how to take care of them. The organization might place them as specialist staff members or may provide them with the amount of work that they can handle. Then, there will always be someone whose pride will be hurt and starts claiming that the organization is now possessed by a demon.

In fact, most of the people who left had similar tendencies. Many of those who were active in the beginning but left, went into a rage or had other reactions seemed to have such tendencies. In this manner, as much as it is important to establish your ego, it should not be too strong either, as it will cause you to lose the power to change yourself.

Hence, the other important thing you need is the sense of public duty. Hold the thought, "It is a good thing if the religious order is moving toward the greatest happiness of the greatest number."

Institutional defense against attacks by evil spirits

Happy Science has always been active as a religious group and recently, we have started doing new things – education, politics and media production such as filmmaking. For some of you in the group, it may have appeared as though the group changed at each occasion. It may even seem as though the group has started something strange. By being unable to adjust to the rapid changes and by trying to overly protect their way of thinking and points of view, those people become detached from the group and eventually end up on the side that criticizes us. In such situations, evil spirits will enter your hearts if you have an unguarded moment.

For instance, staff members who had psychic powers and were offered a stable position within the organization may even go on a rampage because they get furious at the sangha. This may cause even larger scales of demonic forces to take possession.

So, although it can be quite unfortunate for staff members, Happy Science functions differently from the general society by holding a very fluid institutional structure. Unless we do so, staff members place themselves vulnerable to be sniped at by demonic forces.

Thinking about it, when I visited Hokkaido the other day, I said something rude to the chairperson of the board in Happy Science and I'm afraid I have hurt his feelings. I said, "Anybody can be the chairperson." Although I did add, "Within the few chosen people, that is," it was still an unpleasant statement I made [from the lecture, *Ten'i Wo Tadashiku Uketoru Ho* (The Proper Way to Receive the Will of Heaven) at Hokkaido Shoshinkan on July 17, 2014].

A couple of days later, the Happy Science branch assembly was held. Around noon, I felt something approach me. I immediately thought it was an evil spirit and asked who it was, then he started thumping his chest. "Are you the guardian spirit of Mr. XX [the chairperson]?" I asked. Then he said, "Yes, I am." The guardian spirit of the chairperson came to me to ask if I was dissatisfied with him.

The statement I made toward the chairperson may have been a very rude and an embarrassing remark in a secular sense; however, it is just about right to hold bold thoughts such as "anybody can be a chairperson" in order to prevent being struck by demons. If you focus your thoughts and feelings like, "It has to be this particular person to fulfill the role of the chairperson," you will eventually offer moments of vulnerabilities for the demons to strike at you; you will be subjected to focused attack and be beaten down. There have been a number of cases like the example I just raise and those were with people other than the chairperson.

For example, when we only had one editorial division with only one director general, a demon possessed him [in the early years of Happy Science]. The demon tried to "occupy" him since he was the only person who could publish my books. So there was a time when Lucifer possessed the director of the editorial division.

Lucifer also took over the president of IRH Press [in its early years]. In short, if a demon sees that possessing a particular person will lead something to its total destruction, the demon will make that person a target. Then, that person could be defeated. It is for this reason I began to create several people who can carry out certain missions, so that there will be substitutes to cover when it comes down to it. After this personnel system was established, the number of people who were attacked and conquered decreased. This structure may have hurt the pride of some executives, but it is a necessary system of defense as an institution.

Shakyamuni not only had spiritual powers but also The capability to deal with earthly matters

Now, the question was on schizophrenia and multiple personality. Whether a person becomes a psychic or a spiritually disturbed person, similar phenomena will emerge in both cases. Ultimately, it is up to the person's ability to judge, act and work, etc. to see through the legitimacy as well as the good and evil of each case.

There is no danger while the person's management or judgment on practical issues is being carried out fairly and properly. But when some distortion starts to appear, you will need to suspect some kind of spiritual influence. The question, of course, is how to prevent such things from happening. It is crucial to keep cultivating our ability and capacity to respond to worldly matters and circumstances.

I see our lawyer sitting back there [behind the chief editor of *The Liberty*]. I would feel very bad if I only picked on the chief editor, so now let me use our lawyer as an example. If one is a lawyer working at Happy Science, I am guessing there will be times when you feel like you are the greatest lawyer in the world. I do not mind that as much, but if you start saying something like, "I am a lawyer and therefore have been endowed with the 'New Ten Commandments.' A sacred voice from Heaven said to me, 'These are the new laws. You are now the new Moses, spread the new 'Ten Commandments.' Therefore, no other laws are right," there is definitely something ridiculous and unacceptable about that.

Like in this example, there will be something wrong with him as it appears very odd to have extreme leaps. It shows the importance of requiring the capacity to understand and respond to worldly judgments and decisions. In this sense, the state of raising one's spiritual awareness to a certain extent while developing the capacity to respond to worldly matters is desirable.

As Shakyamuni retreated into an ascetic life, he was eventually able to communicate with the spirits of the other world by his endowed psychic powers. But when it came to establishing a religious group, he needed the practical management abilities of this world. Once the religious order was established, arguments and disputes within the group required Shakyamuni to have the ability to arbitrate the quarrels like a judge in court. And when the group became large, Shakyamuni became a political advisor to the king, consulting and offering advice. It can be said that Shakyamuni was able to nurture his practical capabilities adequately and appropriately along with the growth of the religious body.

Therefore, it is important to go through the process properly, step by step. While holding the modest attitude of making effort constantly and aiming to become a reliable person in this world, you should partly make use of spiritual ability if it is given. When one keeps this kind of attitude, he can exert some power of exorcism.

You cannot say that "Prayer for Exorcising Evil Spirits" will work effectively if the person who leads a prayer has absolutely no content. You may say that a person who conduct a prayer is very powerful since he is so "empty" and without content that the void can allow the spirits of the heavenly world to enter him and expel the evil spirits. However, that is not always true as there is something untrustworthy of people with no content. In fact, there are risk and danger when something else could enter the void at a critical moment.

After all, even without the support of any kind of spiritual power, it is important that you have some sort of appropriate judgment as a human entity and enough content to guide others like a school teacher.

Nurture the ability to figure out the truth with Calmness and also establish self-protection

Lastly, we are now left with a case of a person whose personality decayed and has gone completely insane. Unfortunately, in order to become normal, there is only one way left in such situations and that is to be born again. As a matter of fact, there is a point of no return.

There is a following scene in the movie, *The Eternal Zero* [2013]. Before the attack, the protagonist Kyuzo Miyabe, played by Junichi Okada, uses a compass to calculate distances on a map. "If we attack as far as Rabaul and Guadalcanal, we will only have 10 minutes available for air combat. To be in a dogfight is a serious matter and it is not easy at all to finish combat within such short amount of time. It takes 30 minutes, an hour or even longer once the fight starts, so we will fall on our way back. This plan of attack is impossible, it cannot be carried out."

Then the senior officer scolds, "How dare you say that? It is perfectly shameful to speak of defeat before we even start the fight!" I just remember this particular scene. Indeed, there is a point of no return based on cruising distance where one will not be able to turn back and return if he keeps flying.

This also applies in the world of spirituality. Each and every one of us has a "flying range." Even though some people may be able to return even after they approach a certain point, there are others who cannot. It is crucial to have the ability to see through the situation calmly. Among some people, there is a case in which the spirit exits the body, travels to a different planet and then returns to the body. [Refer to Ryuho Okawa, *Chikyu Wo Mamoru Uchu Rengotowa Nanika* (What is the "Galactic Federation" that Protects the Earth?)(Tokyo: IRH Press, 2011).] But if that is to happen to everybody, it is quite likely that most of them will lose their sanity. They will probably be much happier if they didn't experience anything like "traveling to a different planet and coming back." Even if one experiences astral travel, let it be as far as the ceiling of your room. In this sense, "solidifying your own defenses," is necessary.

Afterword

Thirty-three to thirty-four years have already passed since I attained Great Enlightenment in March of 1981 and entered the path of mysticism. If I were to include all the experiences of exorcism against demons, evil spirits and *ikiryo* – evil spirits of living people – the number of times I went through them goes well beyond 5,000. Although I have had difficulty at times, not once have I been defeated.

Nonetheless, there have been few cases in which the soul of a person who was possessed was just too attuned to a demon that the person eventually got dragged to the side of the demon. In addition, if the demon happens to be a demon for over a thousand years, it is most likely for the demon to have a number of worshipers in Hell; although you could drive the demon away, it is an extremely difficult task to guide it to Heaven.

The basic methods to protect yourself from demonic forces are: to not approach them aimlessly, to not have any connections with them and to attune your mind to the vibrations of the heavenly world. Know that there are many cases where the causes of setbacks in life upgrade into the seeds of awakening. It is crucial to never ever let go of your faith.

Ryuho Okawa
Founder and CEO of Happy Science Group
July 31, 2014

ABOUT THE AUTHOR

Founder and CEO of Happy Science Group.

Ryuho Okawa was born on July 7th 1956, in Tokushima, Japan. After graduating from the University of Tokyo with a law degree, he joined a Tokyo-based trading house. While working at its New York headquarters, he studied international finance at the Graduate Center of the City University of New York. In 1981, he attained Great Enlightenment and became aware that he is El Cantare with a mission to bring salvation to all humankind.

In 1986, he established Happy Science. It now has members in over 165 countries across the world, with more than 700 branches and temples as well as 10,000 missionary houses around the world.

He has given over 3,450 lectures (of which more than 150 are in English) and published over 3,000 books (of which more than 600 are Spiritual Interview Series), and many are translated into 40 languages. Along with *The Laws of the Sun* and *The Laws Of Messiah*, many of the books have become best sellers or million sellers. To date, Happy Science has produced 25 movies. The original story and original concept were given by the Executive Producer Ryuho Okawa. He has also composed music and written lyrics of over 450 pieces.

Moreover, he is the Founder of Happy Science University and Happy Science Academy (Junior and Senior High School), Founder and President of the Happiness Realization Party, Founder and Honorary Headmaster of Happy Science Institute of Government and Management, Founder of IRH Press Co., Ltd., and the Chairperson of NEW STAR PRODUCTION Co., Ltd. and ARI Production Co., Ltd.

WHAT IS EL CANTARE?

El Cantare means "the Light of the Earth," and is the Supreme God of the Earth who has been guiding humankind since the beginning of Genesis. He is whom Jesus called Father and Muhammad called Allah, and is *Ame-no-Mioya-Gami*, Japanese Father God. Different parts of El Cantare's core consciousness have descended to Earth in the past, once as Alpha and another as Elohim. His branch spirits, such as Shakyamuni Buddha and Hermes, have descended to Earth many times and helped to flourish many civilizations. To unite various religions and to integrate various fields of study in order to build a new civilization on Earth, a part of the core consciousness has descended to Earth as Master Ryuho Okawa.

Alpha is a part of the core consciousness of El Cantare who descended to Earth around 330 million years ago. Alpha preached Earth's Truths to harmonize and unify Earth-born humans and space people who came from other planets.

Elohim is a part of El Cantare's core consciousness who descended to Earth around 150 million years ago. He gave wisdom, mainly on the differences of light and darkness, good and evil.

Ame-no-Mioya-Gami (Japanese Father God) is the Creator God and the Father God who appears in the ancient literature, *Hotsuma Tsutae*. It is believed that He descended on the foothills of Mt. Fuji about 30,000 years ago and built the Fuji dynasty, which is the root of the Japanese civilization. With justice as the central pillar, Ame-no-Mioya-Gami's teachings spread to ancient civilizations of other countries in the world.

Shakyamuni Buddha was born as a prince into the Shakya Clan in India around 2,600 years ago. When he was 29 years old, he renounced the world and sought enlightenment. He later attained Great Enlightenment and founded Buddhism.

Hermes is one of the 12 Olympian gods in Greek mythology, but the spiritual Truth is that he taught the teachings of love and progress around 4,300 years ago that became the origin of the current Western civilization. He is a hero that truly existed.

Ophealis was born in Greece around 6,500 years ago and was the leader who took an expedition to as far as Egypt. He is the God of miracles, prosperity, and arts, and is known as Osiris in the Egyptian mythology.

Rient Arl Croud was born as a king of the ancient Incan Empire around 7,000 years ago and taught about the mysteries of the mind. In the heavenly world, he is responsible for the interactions that take place between various planets.

Thoth was an almighty leader who built the golden age of the Atlantic civilization around 12,000 years ago. In the Egyptian mythology, he is known as god Thoth.

Ra Mu was a leader who built the golden age of the civilization of Mu around 17,000 years ago. As a religious leader and a politician, he ruled by uniting religion and politics.

ABOUT HAPPY SCIENCE

Happy Science is a global movement that empowers individuals to find purpose and spiritual happiness and to share that happiness with their families, societies, and the world. With more than 12 million members around the world, Happy Science aims to increase awareness of spiritual truths and expand our capacity for love, compassion, and joy so that together we can create the kind of world we all wish to live in.

Activities at Happy Science are based on the Principle of Happiness (Love, Wisdom, Self-Reflection, and Progress). This principle embraces worldwide philosophies and beliefs, transcending boundaries of culture and religions.

Love teaches us to give ourselves freely without expecting anything in return; it encompasses giving, nurturing, and forgiving.

Wisdom leads us to the insights of spiritual truths, and opens us to the true meaning of life and the will of God (the universe, the highest power, Buddha).

Self-Reflection brings a mindful, nonjudgmental lens to our thoughts and actions to help us find our truest selves—the essence of our souls—and deepen our connection to the highest power. It helps us attain a clean and peaceful mind and leads us to the right life path.

Progress emphasizes the positive, dynamic aspects of our spiritual growth—actions we can take to manifest and spread happiness around the world. It's a path that not only expands our soul growth, but also furthers the collective potential of the world we live in.

PROGRAMS AND EVENTS

The doors of Happy Science are open to all. We offer a variety of programs and events, including self-exploration and self-growth programs, spiritual seminars, meditation and contemplation sessions, study groups, and book events.

Our programs are designed to:
* Deepen your understanding of your purpose and meaning in life
* Improve your relationships and increase your capacity to love unconditionally
* Attain peace of mind, decrease anxiety and stress, and feel positive
* Gain deeper insights and a broader perspective on the world
* Learn how to overcome life's challenges
  ... and much more.

For more information, visit happy-science.org.

OUR ACTIVITIES

Happy Science does other various activities to provide support for those in need.

◆ **You Are An Angel! General Incorporated Association**

Happy Science has a volunteer network in Japan that encourages and supports children with disabilities as well as their parents and guardians.

◆ **Never Mind School for Truancy**

At 'Never Mind,' we support students who find it very challenging to attend schools in Japan. We also nurture their self-help spirit and power to rebound against obstacles in life based on Master Okawa's teachings and faith.

◆ **"Prevention Against Suicide" Campaign since 2003**

A nationwide campaign to reduce suicides; over 20,000 people commit suicide every year in Japan. "The Suicide Prevention Website-Words of Truth for You-" presents spiritual prescriptions for worries such as depression, lost love, extramarital affairs, bullying and work-related problems, thereby saving many lives.

◆ **Support for Anti-bullying Campaigns**

Happy Science provides support for a group of parents and guardians, Network to Protect Children from Bullying, a general incorporated foundation launched in Japan to end bullying, including those that can even be called a criminal offense. So far, the network received more than 5,000 cases and resolved 90% of them.

- **The Golden Age Scholarship**
  This scholarship is granted to students who can contribute greatly and bring a hopeful future to the world.

- **Success No.1**
  Buddha's Truth Afterschool Academy
  Happy Science has over 180 classrooms throughout Japan and in several cities around the world that focus on afterschool education for children. The education focuses on faith and morals in addition to supporting children's school studies.

- **Angel Plan V**
  For children under the age of kindergarten, Happy Science holds classes for nurturing healthy, positive, and creative boys and girls.

- **Future Stars Training Department**
  The Future Stars Training Department was founded within the Happy Science Media Division with the goal of nurturing talented individuals to become successful in the performing arts and entertainment industry.

- **NEW STAR PRODUCTION Co., Ltd.**
  ARI Production Co., Ltd.
  We have companies to nurture actors and actresses, artists, and vocalists. They are also involved in film production.

CONTACT INFORMATION

Happy Science is a worldwide organization with branches and temples around the globe. For a comprehensive list, visit the worldwide directory at *happy-science.org*. The following are some of the many Happy Science locations:

UNITED STATES AND CANADA

New York
79 Franklin St., New York, NY 10013, USA
Phone: 1-212-343-7972
Fax: 1-212-343-7973
Email: ny@happy-science.org
Website: happyscience-usa.org

New Jersey
66 Hudson St., #2R, Hoboken, NJ 07030, USA
Phone: 1-201-313-0127
Email: nj@happy-science.org
Website: happyscience-usa.org

Chicago
2300 Barrington Rd., Suite #400,
Hoffman Estates, IL 60169, USA
Phone: 1-630-937-3077
Email: chicago@happy-science.org
Website: happyscience-usa.org

Florida
5208 8th St., Zephyrhills, FL 33542, USA
Phone: 1-813-715-0000
Fax: 1-813-715-0010
Email: florida@happy-science.org
Website: happyscience-usa.org

Atlanta
1874 Piedmont Ave., NE Suite 360-C
Atlanta, GA 30324, USA
Phone: 1-404-892-7770
Email: atlanta@happy-science.org
Website: happyscience-usa.org

San Francisco
525 Clinton St.
Redwood City, CA 94062, USA
Phone & Fax: 1-650-363-2777
Email: sf@happy-science.org
Website: happyscience-usa.org

Los Angeles
1590 E. Del Mar Blvd., Pasadena, CA
91106, USA
Phone: 1-626-395-7775
Fax: 1-626-395-7776
Email: la@happy-science.org
Website: happyscience-usa.org

Orange County
16541 Gothard St. Suite 104
Huntington Beach, CA 92647
Phone: 1-714-659-1501
Email: oc@happy-science.org
Website: happyscience-usa.org

San Diego
7841 Balboa Ave. Suite #202
San Diego, CA 92111, USA
Phone: 1-626-395-7775
Fax: 1-626-395-7776
E-mail: sandiego@happy-science.org
Website: happyscience-usa.org

Hawaii
Phone: 1-808-591-9772
Fax: 1-808-591-9776
Email: hi@happy-science.org
Website: happyscience-usa.org

Kauai
3343 Kanakolu Street, Suite 5
Lihue, HI 96766, USA
Phone: 1-808-822-7007
Fax: 1-808-822-6007
Email: kauai-hi@happy-science.org
Website: happyscience-usa.org

Toronto

845 The Queensway
Etobicoke, ON M8Z 1N6, Canada
Phone: 1-416-901-3747
Email: toronto@happy-science.org
Website: happy-science.ca

Vancouver

#201-2607 East 49th Avenue,
Vancouver, BC, V5S 1J9, Canada
Phone: 1-604-437-7735
Fax: 1-604-437-7764
Email: vancouver@happy-science.org
Website: happy-science.ca

INTERNATIONAL

Tokyo

1-6-7 Togoshi, Shinagawa,
Tokyo, 142-0041, Japan
Phone: 81-3-6384-5770
Fax: 81-3-6384-5776
Email: tokyo@happy-science.org
Website: happy-science.org

Seoul

74, Sadang-ro 27-gil,
Dongjak-gu, Seoul, Korea
Phone: 82-2-3478-8777
Fax: 82-2-3478-9777
Email: korea@happy-science.org
Website: happyscience-korea.org

London

3 Margaret St.
London, W1W 8RE United Kingdom
Phone: 44-20-7323-9255
Fax: 44-20-7323-9344
Email: eu@happy-science.org
Website: www.happyscience-uk.org

Taipei

No. 89, Lane 155, Dunhua N. Road,
Songshan District, Taipei City 105, Taiwan
Phone: 886-2-2719-9377
Fax: 886-2-2719-5570
Email: taiwan@happy-science.org
Website: happyscience-tw.org

Sydney

516 Pacific Highway, Lane Cove North,
2066 NSW, Australia
Phone: 61-2-9411-2877
Fax: 61-2-9411-2822
Email: sydney@happy-science.org

Kuala Lumpur

No 22A, Block 2, Jalil Link Jalan Jalil
Jaya 2, Bukit Jalil 57000,
Kuala Lumpur, Malaysia
Phone: 60-3-8998-7877
Fax: 60-3-8998-7977
Email: malaysia@happy-science.org
Website: happyscience.org.my

Sao Paulo

Rua. Domingos de Morais 1154,
Vila Mariana, Sao Paulo SP
CEP 04010-100, Brazil
Phone: 55-11-5088-3800
Email: sp@happy-science.org
Website: happyscience.com.br

Kathmandu

Kathmandu Metropolitan City,
Ward No. 15, Ring Road, Kimdol,
Sitapaila Kathmandu, Nepal
Phone: 977-1-427-2931
Email: nepal@happy-science.org

Jundiai

Rua Congo, 447, Jd. Bonfiglioli
Jundiai-CEP, 13207-340, Brazil
Phone: 55-11-4587-5952
Email: jundiai@happy-science.org

Kampala

Plot 877 Rubaga Road, Kampala
P.O. Box 34130 Kampala, UGANDA
Phone: 256-79-4682-121
Email: uganda@happy-science.org

HAPPY SCIENCE UNIVERSITY

THE FOUNDING SPIRIT AND THE GOAL OF EDUCATION

Based on the founding philosophy of the university, "Exploration of happiness and the creation of a new civilization," education, research and studies will be provided to help students acquire deep understanding grounded in religious belief and advanced expertise with the objectives of producing "great talents of virtue" who can contribute in a broad-ranging way to serve Japan and the international society.

FACULTIES

Faculty of human happiness

Students in this faculty will pursue liberal arts from various perspectives with a multidisciplinary approach, explore and envision an ideal state of human beings and society.

Faculty of successful management

This faculty aims to realize successful management that helps organizations to create value and wealth for society and to contribute to the happiness and the development of management and employees as well as society as a whole.

Faculty of future creation

Students in this faculty study subjects such as political science, journalism, performing arts and artistic expression, and explore and present new political and cultural models based on truth, goodness and beauty.

Faculty of future industry

This faculty aims to nurture engineers who can resolve various issues facing modern civilization from a technological standpoint and contribute to the creation of new industries of the future.

The Happiness Realization Party (HRP) was founded in May 2009 by Master Ryuho Okawa as part of the Happy Science Group. HRP strives to improve the Japanese society, based on three basic political principles of "freedom, democracy, and faith," and let Japan promote individual and public happiness from Asia to the world as a leader nation.

1) Diplomacy and Security: Protecting Freedom, Democracy, and Faith of Japan and the World from China's Totalitarianism

Japan's current defense system is insufficient against China's expanding hegemony and the threat of North Korea's nuclear missiles. Japan, as the leader of Asia, must strengthen its defense power and promote strategic diplomacy together with the nations which share the values of freedom, democracy, and faith. Further, HRP aims to realize world peace under the leadership of Japan, the nation with the spirit of religious tolerance.

2) Economy: Early economic recovery through utilizing the "wisdom of the private sector"

Economy has been damaged severely by the novel coronavirus originated in China. Many companies have been forced into bankruptcy or out of business. What is needed for economic recovery now is not subsidies and regulations by the government, but policies which can utilize the "wisdom of the private sector."

For more information, visit en.hr-party.jp

ABOUT HS PRESS

HS Press is an imprint of IRH Press Co., Ltd. IRH Press Co., Ltd., based in Tokyo, was founded in 1987 as a publishing division of Happy Science. IRH Press publishes religious and spiritual books, journals, magazines and also operates broadcast and film production enterprises. For more information, visit *okawabooks.com*.

Follow us on:

f Facebook: Okawa Books   ⓘ Instagram: OkawaBooks

▶ Youtube: Okawa Books   🐦 Twitter: Okawa Books

𝓟 Pinterest: Okawa Books   g Goodreads: Ryuho Okawa

——— **NEWSLETTER** ———

To receive book related news, promotions and events, please subscribe to our newsletter below.

🕭 eepurl.com/bsMeJj

——— **AUDIO / VISUAL MEDIA** ———

YOUTUBE

PODCAST

Introduction of Ryuho Okawa's titles; topics ranging from self-help, current affairs, spirituality, religion, and the universe.

BOOKS BY RYUHO OKAWA

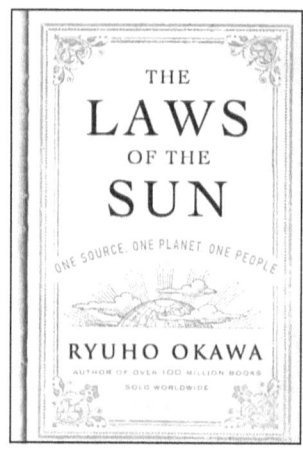

THE LAWS OF THE SUN
ONE SOURCE, ONE PLANET, ONE PEOPLE

ISBN: 978-1-937673-04-8
$24.95 (Hardcover)

IMAGINE IF YOU COULD ASK GOD why He created this world and what spiritual laws He used to shape us—and everything around us. If we could understand His designs and intentions, we could discover what our goals in life should be and whether our actions move us closer to those goals or farther away.

At a young age, a spiritual calling prompted Ryuho Okawa to outline what he innately understood to be universal truths for all humankind. In *The Laws of the Sun*, Okawa outlines these laws of the universe and provides a road map for living one's life with greater purpose and meaning.

In this powerful book, Ryuho Okawa reveals the transcendent nature of consciousness and the secrets of our multidimensional universe and our place in it. By understanding the different stages of love and following the Buddhist Eightfold Path, he believes we can speed up our eternal process of development. *The Laws of the Sun* shows the way to realize true happiness—a happiness that continues from this world through the other.

THE LAWS OF GREAT ENLIGHTENMENT

ALWAYS WALK WITH BUDDHA

ISBN: 978-1-941779-28-6
$14.95 (Paperback)

Buddhist Approaches to Become Stress-Free

In this modern society, people tend to live a stressful life and experience hurting others or being hurt by others. Often they find themselves unable to forgive someone, making it difficult for them to maintain a peaceful mind. However, there are ways to lead a stress-free life and enjoy happiness from within.

This book offers you the practical approaches to achieve it. By understanding the Buddhist concept "enlightenment" described here, you will gain the power to forgive sins and get to know how to be the master of your own mind, not a slave to your emotions.

After reading this book, your view of the world will completely change, and come to understand that we are living in a beautiful world that God created.

THE LAWS OF PERSEVERANCE
REVERSING YOUR COMMON SENSE

ISBN: 978-1-937673-56-7
$14.95 (Paperback)

"No matter how much you suffer, the Truth will gradually shine forth as you continue to endure hardships. Therefore, simply strengthen your mind and keep making constant efforts in times of endurance, however ordinary they may be.

Eventually, you will come out of your slump and overcome your hardships. And, as you try and aim to reverse the common sense, you will one day understand that people can be "undefeated" even if they seem to have lost in this world. In that process, you may sometimes feel that virtue is being generated."

—From Postscript

THE NINE DIMENSIONS

UNVEILING THE LAWS OF ETERNITY

ISBN: 978-0-9826985-6-3
$15.95 (Paperback)

THIS BOOK IS YOUR GATE TO HEAVEN. In this book, Master Okawa shows that God designed this world and the vast, wondrous world of our afterlife as a school with many levels through which our souls learn and grow. This book is a window into the mind of our loving God, who encourages us to grow into greater angels.

SECRETS OF
THE EVERLASTING TRUTHS
A New Paradigm for Living on Earth

ISBN: 978-1-937673-10-9
$14.95 (Paperback)

OUR BELIEF IN THE INVISIBLE IS OUR FUTURE. It is our knowledge about the everlasting spiritual laws and our belief in the invisible that will make it possible for us to solve the world's problems and bring our entire planet together. When you discover the secrets in this book, your view of yourself and the world will be changed dramatically and forever.

"To save the seven billion people on Earth,
God has countless angels working constantly,
every day, on His behalf." —Chapter 3

THE MOMENT OF TRUTH
BECOME A LIVING ANGEL TODAY

ISBN: 978-0-9826985-7-0
$14.95 (Paperback)

MASTER OKAWA shows that we are essentially spiritual beings and that our true and lasting happiness is not found within the material world but rather in acts of unconditional and selfless love toward the greater world. These pages reveal God's mind, His mercy, and His hope that many of us will become living angels that shine light onto this world.

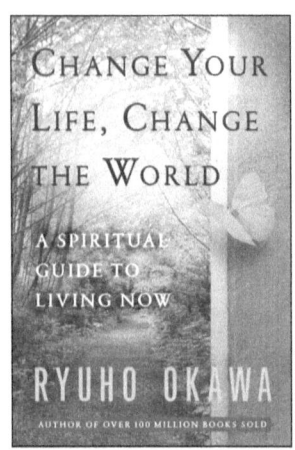

CHANGE YOUR LIFE, CHANGE THE WORLD
A SPIRITUAL GUIDE TO LIVING NOW

ISBN: 978-0-9826985-0-1
$16.95 (Paperback)

MASTER RYUHO OKAWA calls out to people of all nations to remember their true spiritual roots and to build our planet into a united Earth of peace, prosperity, and happiness. With the spiritual wisdom contained in this book, each and every one of us can change our lives and change the world.

THINK BIG!
BE POSITIVE AND BE BRAVE TO ACHIEVE YOUR DREAMS!

ISBN: 978-1-941779-06-4
$14.95 (Paperback)

In *Think Big* Master Ryuho Okawa shares his own philosophy of thinking big, thinking positive, and being brave for
they are essential mindsets in achieving our dreams. While
there is an especial emphasis on developing this philosophy
while we're young, it is universal and valuable for people
of all ages and all walks of life who want to achieve their
dreams and live a successful life. If you do not have any
dreams yet, then this is a must-have book for discovering
why having ideals are an essential part of life. If you already
have aspirations, then discover how to make them come
true. If you are in college, find out valuable tips on how
to get a head start on developing the think big mindset.

ALSO BY RYUHO OKAWA

THE SCIENCE OF HAPPINESS
10 Principles for Manifesting Your Divine Nature

THE GOLDEN LAWS
History through the Eyes of the Eternal Buddha

THE STARTING POINT OF HAPPINESS
A Practical and Intuitive Guide to Discovering Love, Wisdom, and Faith

LOVE, NURTURE, AND FORGIVE
A Handbook to Add a New Richness to Your Life

AN UNSHAKABLE MIND
How to Overcome Life's Difficulties

THE ORIGIN OF LOVE
On the Beauty of Compassion

INVINCIBLE THINKING
There Is No Such Thing as Defeat

GUIDEPOSTS TO HAPPINESS
Prescriptions for a Wonderful Life

THE LAWS OF HAPPINESS
The Four Principles for a Successful Life

TIPS TO FIND HAPPINESS
Creating a Harmonious Home for Your Spouse, Your Children, and Yourself

THE PHILOSOPHY OF PROGRESS
Higher Thinking for Developing Infinite Prosperity

THE ESSENCE OF BUDDHA
The Path to Enlightenment

THE CHALLENGE OF THE MIND
A Practical Approach to the Essential Buddhist Teaching of Karma

THE CHALLENGE OF ENLIGHTENMENT
Realize Your Inner Potential

THE MANIFESTO OF THE HAPPINESS REALIZATION PARTY

RYUHO OKAWA: A POLITICAL REVOLUTIONARY
The Originator of Abenomics and Father of the Happiness Realization Party

SPIRITUAL MESSAGES FROM THE GUARDIAN SPIRIT OF RYUHO OKAWA
The Divine Voice of Shakyamuni Buddha

THE IMPORTANCE OF THE EXPLORATION OF THE RIGHT MIND

INTO THE STORM OF INTERNATIONAL POLITICS
The New Standards of the World Order

HIGHER EDUCATION SERIES

THE NEW IDEA OF A UNIVERSITY
The Groundbreaking Mission of Happy Science University

THE BASIC TEACHINGS OF HAPPY SCIENCE
A Happiness Theory on Truth and Faith

IN LOVE WITH THE SUN
SPIRITUAL MESSAGES FROM GODDESS GAIA

Ryuho Okawa & Shio Okawa

ISBN: 978-1-941779-26-2
$14.95 (Paperback)

After 600 million years, people shall know the true genesis.

The true story when the earth was born, The guiding concept of the earth, The mechanism of creating life on Earth. And the future that human beings has to seek, These secrets are now revealed by the spiritual message from Goddess Gaia, Who supported the creation of Earth civilization by Alpha, the God of origin.

Through reading this book, you will see the magnificent scale of El Cantare's Law.

"I would like for you to listen to the bell ringing the advent of a spiritual revolution."

— Ryuho Okawa, Preface

THE TRUTH OF THE PACIFIC WAR
SOULFUL MESSAGES FROM HIDEKI TOJO,
JAPAN'S WARTIME LEADER

ISBN: 978-1-941779-22-4
$14.95 (Paperback)

In this book, we provide you with the material needed to rethink whether or not the perception of World War II by the winners was right, through looking back on history starting with the current world affairs. This is all necessary for us to get a thorough understanding of ongoing confusion in the world and to seek the path of peace, stability and progress of future humankind.

The material provided is a new testimony by General Hideki Tojo, who is enshrined at Yasukuni Shrine and who was Japan's most significant figure in the Pacific War. Furthermore, we have also recorded a testimony by Supreme Commander of the Allied Powers Douglas MacArthur in order to ensure a fair argument.

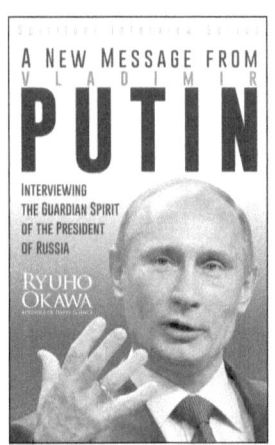

A NEW MESSAGE FROM VLADIMIR PUTIN

INTERVIEWING THE GUARDIAN SPIRIT OF THE PRESIDENT OF RUSSIA

ISBN: 978-1-937673-94-9
$14.95 (Paperback)

We hereby bring you the most recent spiritual message from the guardian spirit of President Putin, the politician who is the center of attention of not just the people of Russia but of the whole world, regardless of it being in a good or a bad way. In the Preface, it says, "President Putin's true intentions, which are 90 percent misunderstood."

We hope that, through this book, the reader will come to understand the true thoughts of Mr. Putin which are still undisclosed to the public. And, we hope that the reader will foresee the new world order that this skilled politician is thinking of, and make use of that in predicting how the international affairs will turn out in the future.

THE SECRET BEHIND
"THE RAPE OF NANKING"
A SPIRITUAL CONFESSION BY IRIS CHANG

ISBN: 978-1-941779-08-8
$9.95 (Paperback)

Sometimes a single book can determine how the international society sees history, as well as give a great impact on international relations. If a fabricated history had spread throughout the world and is subjecting the citizens of a particular country to humiliation that they don't deserve, then speaking from international justice and humanitarian viewpoints, such history must be rewritten in an objective and impartial manner. There is a phrase, "History is written by the victors." The usual process is that, after a war, the victors come up with a one-sided historical view that is advantageous to them and historical researchers of later generations gradually make corrections to it.

Nevertheless, sometimes history takes a sudden turn due to revelations from Heaven. This book is a rare example of that. The author of a book which gave a great impact on the historical view that had spread throughout the international society today confessed the truth regarding the content of her book and its background, just 10 years after her death, in a form of a spiritual message.

THE GENIUS OF ICHIRO
THE SECRET BEHIND HIS FOUR THOUSAND HITS

ISBN: 978-1-941779-04-0
$14.95 (Paperback)

Ichiro Suzuki arrived in Seattle in 2001 as a mostly anonymous free agent from Japan's NPB, and while there was buzz about his potential, no one really knew what to expect. Since then, he has set many records in American Major League Baseball, including the record for most hits in a single season (262) and longest streak of two-hundred-hit seasons (ten years). On August 21, 2013, he got the four thousandth hit of his professional baseball career. This spiritual interview reveals the "making of Ichiro," including the secrets to his professionalism, his techniques for overcoming slumps, and how he made it to the top. The interview highlights Ichiro's unique traits that continue to impress us, twelve years after he first unleashed the laser beam.

124

ON HAPPINESS REVOLUTION
A SPIRITUAL INTERVIEW WITH HANNAH ARENDT

ISBN: 978-1-937673-82-6
$14.95 (Paperback)

Since 2010, Master Ryuho Okawa has published over two hundred spiritual messages, in Japanese, from the spirits of historical men and women and the guardian spirits of today's living figures. With this Spiritual Interview Series, Master Okawa is now making these important messages available in English. The books in this series are messages from the spirits or guardian spirits of people who have a great deal of influence over world affairs. These messages reveal these powerful figures' hidden intentions and disclose facts that even news reporters would have difficulty drawing out. Master Okawa's in-depth analyses of these messages give us the tools that we need to understand and confront the dangers that lie ahead of us. Master Okawa hopes to show readers that the spirit world and spirits are real, and that by understanding spiritual truths, we can bring a peaceful end to international conflicts and create solutions to a variety of global crises.

ARE ISLAMIC EXTREMISTS
JIHADISTS OR TERRORISTS?
THE NECESSITY OF FREEDOM IN ISLAMIC COUNTRIES

ISBN: 978-1-941779-14-9

$14.95 (Paperback)

The West has been leading a long war on terror since the 9/11 terrorist attacks in 2001 on American soil by Osama bin Laden's al-Qaeda. Even after the assassination of Osama bin Laden on May 2, 2011, by President Obama's Special Forces unit, terrorist attacks have continued around the world. On January 16, 2013, an international crisis erupted when Islamic terrorists organized by Mokhtar Belmokhtar lay siege to an Algerian gas plant. After the Algerian government sent in a special forces unit, thirty-nine foreign hostages were killed and 685 Algerian workers and one hundred foreigners escaped or were freed.*

Are the attacks by Islamic extremist groups like al-Qaeda and the organization led by Mokhtar Belmokhtar unjust acts of terror? Or are they justified acts of a holy war, as the self-proclaimed jihadists claim? In this interview with Osama bin Laden, Master Ryuho Okawa provides us with his conclusive answer to these questions.

* "Q&A: Hostage Crisis in Algeria," BBC News, January 21, 2013, http://www.bbc.com/news/world-africa-21056884.

LEADERSHIP SECRETS OF LIU BANG
THE EMPEROR OF CHINA'S HAN DYNASTY
WITH A SURPRISING CONNECTION WITH STEVEN SPIELBERG

ISBN: 978-1-941779-17-0
$14.95 (Paperback)

Liu Bang, also known as Gaozu, began from humble peasant roots and served as a police officer under the Qin dynasty. He rose through the ranks, first receiving control of western China, and eventually becoming the ruler of China as the founder and first emperor of the Han dynasty (206 BCE–220 CE). The histories of kings and rulers often provide valuable lessons about the universal principles that can be applied to today's management, entrepreneurship, and all types of large undertakings. As this spiritual interview has shown, Liu Bang's strengths and achievements are marked by a strong global element. Everyone who aspires to lead a large organization can learn from his ability to win people's hearts. You may be surprised to discover that this long-ago emperor of China is living today in the United States as one of the world's most famous film directors, Steven Spielberg.

THE TRUTH OF NANKING AND COMFORT WOMEN ISSUES
A Spiritual Reading Into World War II
by Edgar Cayce

ISBN: 978-1-937673-86-4
$14.95 (Paperback)

Did the so-called "Nanking Massacre" and the military comfort women forcefully taken by the Japanese troops actually exist as historical facts? In this book, we attempt to investigate whether the two events actually took place by using a new method. This is not merely to restore the international honor of Japan. We are hoping to review the causes of World War II, look over the world justice made by the victorious nations after the war and reveal the true world history.

THE NEW DIPLOMATIC STRATEGIES
OF SIR WINSTON CHURCHILL

A SPIRITUAL INTERVIEW WITH THE FORMER PRIME MINISTER
REGARDING THE AGE OF PERSEVERANCE

ISBN: 978-1-937673-85-7
$14.95 (Paperback)

Today, two politicians are criticized and compared to Hitler; President Vladimir Putin of Russia and Prime Minister Shinzo Abe of Japan. Are these politicians really dangerous to be likened to Hitler? Or, just like in Hitler's case, can it be that another truly dangerous politician exists in another country that is yet to be discovered? If there is a chance to hear the opinion of Sir Winston Churchill, considered to be Hitler's arch enemy, journalists around the world would probably be interested to hear this. The series on Spiritual Messages by Ryuho Okawa, Happy Science, made this possible. This book contains a record of an interview conducted with the spirit of former British Prime Minister Churchill by Master Okawa in March this year. It is a record of an interview on issues related to the "next appearance of Hitler," and on current international affairs.

THE ART OF BUSINESS REVITALIZATION
MANAGEMENT WISDOM FROM JACK WELCH, CARLOS GHOSN, AND BILL GATES

ISBN: 978-1-937673-70-3
$19.95 (Paperback)

In *The Art of Business Revitalization: Management Wisdom from Jack Welch*, Carlos Ghosn, and Bill Gates, Master Ryuho Okawa conducts spiritual interviews with three of the greatest executives of our time. General Electric's Jack Welch, Renault and Nissan's Carlos Ghosn, and Microsoft's Bill Gates give readers a glimpse into how they took hold of opportunities and turned them into successes. What management philosophies helped Jack Welch and Carlos Ghosn turn around their companies during downturns? What is Bill Gates's secret to creating products that become global standards? What human resources management and education philosophies have they drawn upon to keep their companies at the top? This book reveals the secrets to their achievements.

For a complete list of books in the Spiritual Interview Series, visit spiritualinterview.com

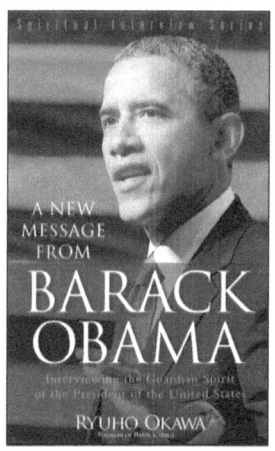

A NEW MESSAGE FROM
BARACK OBAMA
INTERVIEWING THE GUARDIAN SPIRIT OF
THE PRESIDENT OF THE UNITED STATES

ISBN: 978-1-937673-89-5
$14.95 (Paperback)

In April 2014, President Obama embarked on his fifth trip to Asia during his time in office to discuss the pressing issues in the Asia-pacific region. A week before his Asia trip, Master Ryuho Okawa held a spiritual interview with Barack Obama, which revealed his true objectives of his Asia tour and about his thoughts on current affairs in the world. What is President Obama's vision of America's role in the world today? Why does he believe that America is not the world's policeman? This spiritual interview reveals President Obama's stance on international relations including America's relationship with China, the Ukraine crisis and Islamic extremism. It also discloses his honest feelings about Japanese Prime Minister Abe and Russian President Putin. Now that America is "on the verge of crisis," as the guardian spirit of President Obama says in this interview, we all need to think about how we can achieve security, justice and peace in the world without the "world's policeman."

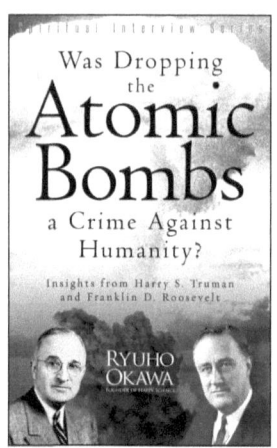

WAS DROPPING THE ATOMIC BOMBS A CRIME AGAINST HUMANITY?

INSIGHTS FROM HARRY S. TRUMAN AND FRANKLIN D. ROOSEVELT

ISBN: 978-1-937673-78-9
$14.95 (Paperback)

Was there any true justification for the atomic bombing of Hiroshima and Nagasaki? To answer to this question, Master Ryuho Okawa conducted spiritual interviews with Harry S. Truman and Franklin D. Roosevelt, the two presidents who presided over the United States' participation in World War II. Could anything justify the use of nuclear weapons on civilians? Was Pearl Harbor really a sneak attack, or did Franklin Roosevelt know of it beforehand? This book reveals valuable information that will help the world gain a truthful understanding of world history.

JAPAN! REGAIN YOUR
SAMURAI SPIRIT

A Message from the Guardian Spirit of Lee Teng-hui,
Former President of the Republic of China

IISBN: 978-1-937673-77-2
$14.95 (Paperback)

This book is the record of interviews conducted on Former President of Taiwan Lee Teng-hui's subconscious
[guardian spirit] in February 2014. His true thoughts, as
well as the truth on modern East-Asian history, were revealed in these interviews. The book is filled with hints
on how to give another thought to the causes of World
War II. As it is stated in the afterword, this is a book
which we want "all politicians, all people in the media, and everyone who talks about politics" to read.

DIPLOMATIC STRATEGY FOR JAPAN, U.S. AND CHINA

A Message from the Guardian Spirit of Diplomatic Analyst Hisahiko Okazaki

ISBN: 978-1-937673-75-8
$14.95 (Paperback)

This book contains the interview conducted with the guardian spirit of former diplomat, Hisahiko Okazaki, a conservative commentator representative to Japan. An astonishing relation between Admiral Perry and Okazaki is revealed in this interview. By reading this book, you will come to know what Admiral Perry thinks on the current situation of the world, and the relation between Japan and the United States, 160 years later since he opened up Japan which was in seclusion.

WHY I AM ANTI-JAPAN
INTERVIEWING THE GUARDIAN SPIRIT OF KOREAN PRESIDENT PARK GEUN-HYE

ISBN: 978-1-937673-67-3
$14.95 (Paperback)

This book is the record of interviews conducted on President Park's subconscious [guardian spirit] in February 2014, which were done in order to find out the fundamental reason to her anti-Japanese sentiments. Her true thoughts, as well as the truth on modern Japan-Korea history, were revealed in these interviews. By having numerous people in the world know of this truth, starting with the Japanese, South Koreans, Americans and the Chinese, the path to create a constructive future of the Pacific Basin should open as we resolve the conflicting emotions between Japan and South Korea in the international society.

A WARNING TO
SOUTH KOREA'S PRESIDENT
WORDS FROM HER FATHER,
FORMER PRESIDENT PARK CHUNG-HEE

ISBN: 978-1-937673-65-9
$14.95 (Paperback)

Park Chung-hee served as the president of the Republic of Korea (South Korea) for almost sixteen years, from 1963 until his death in 1979. Today, people around the world know him as the assassinated father of Park Geun-hye, the current and first female president of South Korea. In this spiritual interview, Park Chung-hee's spirit shares his opinions on the roles of South Korea, Japan, the United States, China, and North Korea in the global context. What are his thoughts on the Takeshima island dispute, the comfort-women issue, China's future prospects, and the direction South Korea should take as a country? A Warning to South Korea's President is a father's message to his daughter as he seeks to guide their nation in the right direction. This interview lets us see history in a new light and shows us how to build a better future for the Asia-Pacific region.

INTERVIEWING THE GUARDIAN SPIRIT OF U.S. AMBASSADOR CAROLINE KENNEDY

A NEW BRIDGE BETWEEN JAPAN AND THE U.S.

ISBN: 978-1-937673-63-5
$14.95 (Paperback)

CONTENTS

1 Caroline's Guardian Spirit Makes an "Informal" Appearance
2 Her View on Japan-U.S. and Japan-China Relations
3 True Emotions Behind America's Disappointment in Yasukuni Visit
4 World War II
5 Comfort Women Issue and Women's Rights
6 The Reason Behind the Kennedy Tragedies
7 Drive-Hunt Dolphin Killing, and Japanese vs. American Cultures
8 Japanese Princess and Roman Emperor in Past Lives?
9 Message to Japan

FOR THE FUTURE OF
THAILAND AND JAPAN

INTERVIEWING THE GUARDIAN SPIRIT OF
YINGLUCK SHINAWATRA

ISBN: 978-1-937673-59-8
$14.95 (Paperback)

In December 2013, Thailand's Prime Minister Yingluck announced the dissolution of the nation's parliament and called a snap election to be held in February 2014. But this did not appease the thousands of angry protestors who remained on the streets of Bangkok. During this time of social unrest, Prime Minister Yingluck were mostly absent from Bangkok to avoid protestors, spending more time in the Northern and Northeastern areas. It was in such a difficult time for the prime minister and the country of Thailand that Master Ryuho Okawa conducted a spiritual interview with Prime Minister Yingluck. In this spiritual interview, the guardian spirit of Prime Minister Yingluck shares her views on many controversial topics including democracy in Thailand, Thailand's relationships with China and Japan, traditional Buddhism, and Islam. She then asks Japan to help her country which has plunged into turmoil. It is Master Ryuho Okawa's hope that this interview will become a bridge to build a wonderful relationship between Thailand and Japan.

MOTHER TERESA'S CURRENT CALLING IN HEAVEN

THE SAINT OF THE GUTTERS DELIVERS HER EXPERIENCES OF
GOD, HEAVEN, AND OUR MISSION

ISBN: 978-1-937673-55-0
$14.95 (Paperback)

This book is a spiritual interview with Mother Teresa's spirit who talks through Master Ryuho Okawa. In this spiritual interview, which was conducted sixteen years after Mother Teresa's death, Mother Teresa's spirit talks about her astonishing discoveries about God, Heaven, and the mission that people on earth should aim to fulfill through life. Mother Teresa reveals that the other world is a vast place with many levels of angels, that Heaven and Hell exist, and that the reality of the human being is the soul. In addition to a discussion about the contradictions within Christian teachings and the need for new teachings for today's people, she also talks about her discoveries about God and Jesus Christ, and says that it is the mission of the wealthy to help others who are in poverty, through prayer and a pure heart.

NELSON MANDELA'S LAST MESSAGE

A Conversation with Madiba
Six Hours After His Death

ISBN: 978-1-937673-53-6
$14.95 (Paperback)

On December 5, 2013, the entire world mourned the passing of Nelson Mandela. Even as the news was spreading, Mandela's spirit came to Master Ryuho Okawa to give us all an important message of hope and to prove that the afterlife exists. Archbishop of Canterbury Justin Wilby paid this tribute to the first black president of South Africa and the man who liberated his country from apartheid: "His courage was undefeated, indomitable, extraordinary." Perhaps it was Mandela's indomitable belief in the fundamental reality of the human soul that gave him such extraordinary courage in the face of adversity. For as he says in this spiritual interview, God created our souls as thinking energy without color, and that our colorless soul is the basis of our fundamental freedom and equality. In this spiritual interview, Master Ryuho Okawa gives us a glimpse into the mind of this great leader whose undefeated spirit is a message of hope to us all.

SOUTH KOREA'S CONSPIRACY
PRESIDENT PARK'S HIDDEN AGENDA TO UNITE WITH CHINA

ISBN: 978-1-937673-51-2
$14.95 (Paperback)

On June 27, 2013, South Korea's President Park Geun-hye and Chinese President Xi Jinping held summit talks in Beijing. At the meeting, President Park asked China's Xi Jinping to build a memorial of An Jung-geun, the man who in 1909 assassinated the first Prime Minister of Japan and the first Resident-General of Korea, Ito Hirobumi. In this spiritual interview, we begin by speaking with the spirit of An Jung-geun before moving on to a conversation with the guardian spirit of President Park, who forced herself into the interview out of fear that the interview will reveal the truth about him. Through these conversations, Master Ryuho Okawa tries to discover the facts about the assassination of Ito Hirobumi to determine whether An Jung-geun can justifiably be hailed as a hero. While South Koreans continue to accuse Japan of having wronged their nation, Master Okawa hopes that these interviews will provide a truthful understanding of the historical events between Japan and South Korea and help the international community understand the nature of true international justice.

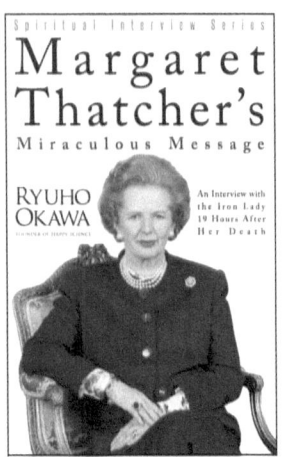

MARGARET THATCHER'S
MIRACULOUS MESSAGE
AN INTERVIEW WITH THE IRON LADY
19 HOURS AFTER HER DEATH

ISBN: 978-1-937673-37-6
$14.95 (Paperback)

On April 9, 2013, just nineteen hours after Margaret Thatcher's death, Master Ryuho Okawa summoned her spirit to hold a miraculous spiritual interview with Europe's first female prime minister, famously known as the Iron Lady. In words marked by her signature clarity and determination, Margaret Thatcher provided valuable answers to essential and timely questions. Her answers will prove helpful not only to the United Kingdom, but also to the global economy and governments all over the world, including those of the United States and the European Union.

UNMASKING BAN KI-MOON'S BIASED STANCE

INVESTIGATING THE PARALYSIS OF THE UNITED NATIONS

ISBN: 978-1-937673-49-9
$14.95 (Paperback)

The world is currently facing many critical international issues that require resolution through strong leadership dedicated to the preservation of international peace and security. What are U.N. Secretary-General Ban Ki-moon's true thoughts on these pressing issues? What does he think about the disputes between Japan and South Korea over ownership of the Takeshima Islands, between Japan and China over ownership of the Senkaku Islands, and between Iran and Israel over nuclear weapons capability? Can we depend on him to successfully uphold the principle of impartiality in the United Nations's role of peacemaking? In this spiritual interview with the guardian spirit of Mr. Ban Ki-moon, Master Okawa reveals the U.N. Secretary-General's true character and true intentions regarding his important peacemaking responsibilities.

STEVE JOBS RETURNS
WITH HIS SECRETS
BE SIMPLE, BE CRAZY

ISBN: 978-1-937673-47-5
$19.95 (Paperback)

In this spiritual interview with Steve Jobs, conducted just three months after his death, Master Okawa offers us a chance to catch a glimpse into the mind of one of America's modern geniuses, whom President Barack Obama has described as one among the greatest American innovators. What was the aesthetic philosophy behind his passionate drive to create products that he described as "at the intersection of art and technology?" What were the secrets to his creativity and the successful sales of his products? As Master Okawa often says, and as this interview with the mind of one of the greatest modern innovators will show you, success is always in the way we think and in the substance of our goals and ideals.

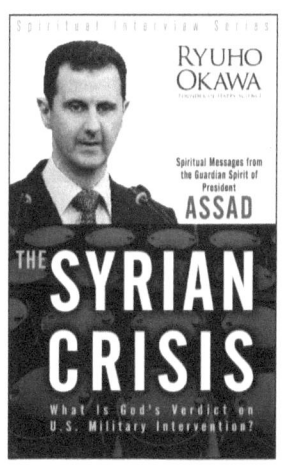

THE SYRIAN CRISIS

WHAT IS GOD'S VERDICT ON U.S. MILITARY INTERVENTION?

ISBN: 978-1-937673-44-4
$14.95 (Paperback)

Is there justice in a U.S. military intervention into the ongoing Syrian crisis? What is God's perspective on the tragedy that is occurring in Syria? In *The Syrian Crisis: What Is God's Verdict on U.S. Military Intervention?* Master Ryuho Okawa conducts a spiritual interview with the guardian spirit of Bashar al-Assad. As this interview reveals, the Syrian dictator's true character is quite different from what we saw in the CBS interview. As the world braces for a possible world war, Master Ryuho Okawa provides us with a clear sense of where God's justice lies in this international crisis.

THE JUST CAUSE IN THE IRAQ WAR

DID SADDAM HUSSEIN POSSESS
WEAPONS OF MASS DESTRUCTION?

ISBN: 978-1-937673-41-3
$14.95 (Paperback)

The Just Cause in the Iraq War: Did Saddam Hussein Possess Weapons of Mass Destruction? tackles one of the most controversial and pertinent issues in international politics today. Is President Obama correct that the Iraq War was an unjust war, as he claimed during the 2012 presidential race? Did Saddam Hussein truly have no weapons of mass destruction, or are those weapons still hidden in Iraq, somewhere beyond the reach of U.S. intelligence? In this book, you will discover that Saddam Hussein was also behind the planning of the 9/11 terrorist attacks and both he and Osama bin Laden are now in Hell. The knowledge this book provides will help each of us make the right decisions as we work together to create a peaceful international society.

FORECASTING THE SECOND KOREAN WAR
HOW WILL THE WORLD HANDLE THE CRISIS?

ISBN: 978-1-937673-35-2
$14.95 (Paperback)

Forecasting the Second Korean War: How Will the World Handle the Crisis? forecasts a potential crisis that the United States, South Korea, and Japan may face. In part 1, Master Okawa draws on the help of Edgar Cayce to describe in detail the unfolding of a second Korean War that could begin in the summer of 2013. Part 2 of this book contains a spiritual interview with Kim Il Sung that reveals that he is spiritually guiding Kim Jong Un. Together, the two parts of this book reveal the shocking fact that the crisis on the Korean peninsula is only a small part of a larger and more global imperialistic scheme that is being masterminded by Xi Jinping, the president of China. You will discover who is truly behind the Islamist terrorist attacks against the United States.

EXPOSING NORTH KOREA'S MENACING LEADER

KIM JONG UN'S PLOT FOR A PSYCHOLOGICAL WAR

ISBN: 978-1-937673-39-0
$14.95 (Paperback)

Exposing North Korea's Menacing Leader: Kim Jong Un's Plot for a Psychological War reveals the role that North Korea is playing in China's imperialistic strategy and the two nations' close ties with Iran. Together, China and Kim Jong Un—North Korea's supreme leader— are carrying out a psychological war that takes full advantage of the weaknesses of Japanese Prime Minister Abe and United States President Obama. Indeed, this interview with Kim Jong Un's guardian spirit reveals that Kim Jong Un was most likely behind the Boston marathon bombings that occurred on April 15, 2013.

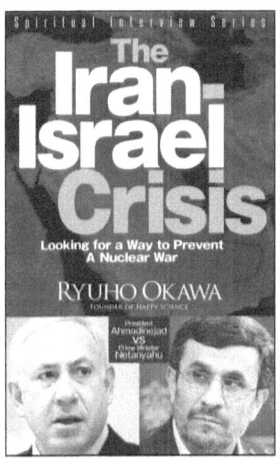

THE IRAN-ISRAEL CRISIS

LOOKING FOR A WAY TO PREVENT A NUCLEAR WAR

ISBN: 978-1-937673-26-0
$14.95 (Paperback)

Master Ryuho Okawa firmly believes that the power to create lasting global peace will come from embracing love and forgiveness beyond differences in religion. This set of spiritual interviews with the guardian spirits of Iran's President Mahmoud Ahmadinejad and Israel's Prime Minister Benjamin Netanyahu reveal their living counterparts' underlying ideas about each other's nations as arch enemies. You will discover hints to solving long-standing clashes between religions.

CHINA'S SECRET MILITARY BASES

A REMOTE-VIEWING INVESTIGATION
OF SUSPICIOUS SATELLITE IMAGES

ISBN: 978-1-937673-24-6
$14.95 (Paperback)

Master Okawa reveals China's versions of Area 51 from mysterious satellite photos that had aroused worldwide curiosity. Even American intelligence will be shocked to find out these truths about a hidden enormous missile-launching site full of nuclear warheads prepared to strike major cities around the world. This book is a must-read for anyone who wants to save the world from a full-out nuclear war.

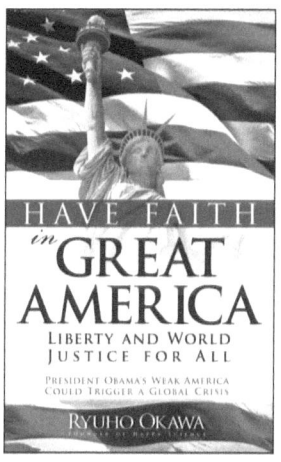

HAVE FAITH IN GREAT AMERICA
LIBERTY AND WORLD JUSTICE FOR ALL

ISBN: 978-1-937673-20-8
$14.95 (Paperback)

Have Faith in Great America: Liberty and World Justice for All is Master Ryuho Okawa's earnest message to the United States of America. The world's future depends on America's fulfillment of its long-held sacred mission of protecting the faith, liberty, and justice of people and nations around the world, and on the development of strong bonds between the United States and Japan.

CHINA'S HIDDEN AGENDA
THE MASTERMIND BEHIND THE ANTI-AMERICAN
AND ANTI-JAPANESE PROTESTS

ISBN: 978-1937673-18-5
$14.95 (Paperback)

"Anti-American demonstrations have been raging in over twenty Arab countries. The man pulling the strings behind all this is Xi Jinping."

—Master Ryuho Okawa

"I wanted to stir up the anti-American movement in the Arab world to make sure that the United States won't be able to attack Syria or Iran...I'm the mastermind behind the Muhammad video."

—Xi Jinping's Guardian Spirit

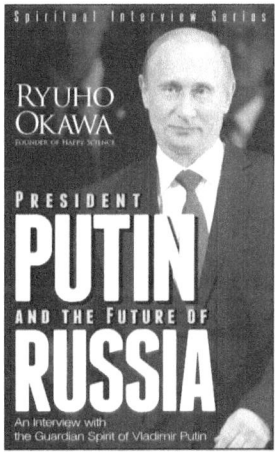

PRESIDENT PUTIN AND THE FUTURE OF RUSSIA

AN INTERVIEW WITH THE GUARDIAN SPIRIT OF VLADIMIR PUTIN

ISBN: 978-1-937673-14-7
$14.95 (Paperback)

"I have no intention of fighting the United States. The Cold War is over... I have no intention of fighting the Americans... And I'm not friendly enough with China to think about joining them against the United States... I have given Russians religious freedom, which makes me very different from the Chinese."

—Putin's Guardian Spirit

www.ingramcontent.com/pod-product-compliance
Lightning Source LLC
Chambersburg PA
CBHW030305130626
46549CB00002B/703